ATTITUDES AND INTERESTS
IN EDUCATION

ATTITUDES AND INTERESTS IN EDUCATION

by

K. M. EVANS

B.SC., M.A., PH.D. (LOND.)

Reader in Education, University College, Cardiff

Routledge & Kegan Paul

LONDON AND BOSTON

First published 1965
by Routledge & Kegan Paul Limited
Broadway House, 68-74 Carter Lane
London, EC4V 5EL
and 9 Park Street
Boston, Mass, 02108 U.S.A.

Reprinted and first published
as a Routledge Paperback 1971

Reprinted 1972 (*twice*)

Printed in Great Britain
by Unwin Brothers Limited
The Gresham Press, Old Woking
Surrey, England

ISBN 0 7100 1345 0 (*c*)
ISBN 0 7100 7166 3 (*p*)

CONTENTS

PREFACE

AS BEFITS THE IMPORTANCE of the subject, the field of attitude and interest research is extremely wide, and no one book could cover it in its entirety. This book does not claim to be exhaustive, but it is hoped that it gives an adequate introduction to some of the experimental work which has been carried out since about 1930.

A much clearer appreciation of the value of experimental work is possible when the reader understands how the qualities considered have been assessed, and this is one reason why methods of assessment of attitudes and interests have been described in some detail. A second reason for the inclusion of this more technical work is that there is a growing body of students and teachers engaged in advanced work in University Institutes and Departments of Education, many of whom make experimental studies of the attitudes and interests of school children. They need an accessible account of methods suitable for their purposes and it is hoped that this book will be of use to them.

It is also hoped that it will be of interest to the much larger body of teachers who are concerned about their pupils and who want to help them to grow up to be useful and happy members of society. Whether they do so or not will depend very much on the attitudes and interests they acquire before they leave school. Intentionally or not, all of us who are teachers are influencing the attitudes of our pupils and we should be aware of this. We teach far more than the subject matter of our lessons, and if we are conscious of the ways we

Preface

are doing this, we are more likely to bring about the ends we desire than if we trust to blind intuition. Hit or miss is not good enough in education. It is wasteful of effort and uncertain of result.

There is no intention of imposing the author's ideas of what are desirable attitudes and interests for teachers to encourage in their pupils. Decisions of good and bad are value decisions, and, as such, are the province of the philosopher, not the psychologist. The psychologist's function is to provide information about whether, in given circumstances, particular attitudes and interests can be developed or changed, and to show how these results can be achieved. It is for individual teachers to apply this information to the circumstances of their own classrooms, and to use it in educating their pupils as they think they should be educated. Readymade solutions to problems in education rarely fit real cases, and some do-it-yourself is always necessary. It is not necessary, though, to start from scratch every time, and other people's experience can provide useful clues.

That is why it has been thought good to give accounts of ways in which some classroom problems have been investigated. Much of the work described was done by teachers, so it is more obviously relevant to school work than laboratory experiments sometimes appear to be, and may be more easily adapted for use in other schools.

In writing this book, the author has benefited, more than they perhaps realised, from discussions, over a number of years, of a group of experienced teachers. They helped to ensure that theory and practice did not part company too often. Help is also gratefully acknowledged from Dr. C. M. Fleming, who read the whole of the manuscript, and from Dr. J. P. Spillane and Dr. D. L. Davies, who read parts of it. All provided comments and criticism which have been most valuable. They should not, however, be considered responsible for any errors which may have crept in, and for these the author alone must be blamed.

Finally, it is with much pleasure that the author takes this

Preface

opportunity of expressing, once again, gratitude and appreciation for assistance from the staff of the Library of the University College of South Wales and Monmouthshire. Without this, it would have been quite impossible to trace and check the very large number of works referred to in writing a book of this nature.

K.M.E.

Cardiff, 1965.

I

INTRODUCTION

ASK A BOY what he learns at school and he will tell you English and mathematics, history and geography, science and languages. But his teachers, if not the boy himself, will know that he learns far more than this. Modes of thinking and acting, attitudes and interests are also acquired and developed during school days, and these may become permanent, remaining effective and observable long after the greater part of the subject matter learnt has been overlaid or forgotten.

It would be difficult to overstress the influence of attitudes and interests in the lives of individual people. They determine what a man will do or say in particular situations, what he will enjoy or dislike, his approach to other people, and his reactions to events in his own life and in the world around. The expression of attitudes, either in actions or in words, provides clues to personality and to needs, and makes possible the kind of understanding which is necessary for the formation of stable relationships. One can know very little about a person who never expresses an opinion or shows any interest.

On the social level, by holding the 'correct' opinions an individual can identify with a group and can be seen to belong to it. Equally, he may dissociate himself from a group to which he is opposed or be rejected by it on the basis of his opinions. The group may be a political party, a social class, an athletics club, a school or a family, but, whatever it is, if an individual wishes to live comfortably within it, he will find this easier if he obviously holds opinions current among the members and behaves in the 'right' way. To be acceptable, it is often necessary to conform to group standards.

1

Introduction

Then, too, attitudes provide patterns of behaviour. Without some readymade responses to call upon, we should have to consider each situation in which we found ourselves as it occurred and decide every time how to act. Attitudes which come into play automatically in appropriate circumstances avoid this necessity and aid us in taking prompt action, much as a knowledge of the basic number facts aids in the solution of an arithmetical problem.

Interests are less strictly utilitarian than attitudes but they are important none the less. Interest involves feelings rather than beliefs, and interests are what make life worth living, while the lack of interests may lead to a sterile and despairing existence. The child who does not want to do anything in particular and the retired business man who cannot occupy his time are pitiable creatures, and probably both are heading for disaster. Happily, most children have a lively curiosity and it is not difficult to catch or arouse their interest. To help them to find and develop satisfying interests is one of the most worthwhile tasks in teaching.

Inculcating attitudes and interests and aiding their growth is an important part of education, but it involves a type of problem less frequently encountered in teaching the subjects of the curriculum. Any school subject is concerned with a body of knowledge which the children must learn. This has to be selected from the total of knowledge, for its usefulness, or because it is necessary as a preliminary to further learning, or just because it is attractive in itself. In the main, there is no moral question involved for a teacher in drawing up a syllabus in mathematics or a language. When it comes to attitudes, however, there is a moral problem in deciding what the children should learn. Society approves some attitudes but not others. There is a question of correct or incorrect in an academic subject, but of good or bad where attitudes are concerned, and this is an added responsibility for the teacher. How should one decide what attitudes a child should hold towards himself, to authority or to foreigners? And who should make the decision?

Introduction

There is a similar question related to interests. Children must be encouraged to be interested in what is true, beautiful and of good report, not in what is evil. They must learn to enjoy creation, not destruction, health not disease. It is probably easier to see what is good and what is bad here than in the case of attitudes, but it is not safe to assume that we automatically 'needs must love the highest when we see it.' We usually have to be taught to see it and learn to recognise it for what it is, and then we may begin to love it.

Fortunately, attitudes and interests can be and are learned. What form they will take is not determined at birth or earlier, but depends on the environment in which the child grows up and the treatment he receives. We do not really know how children acquire the value-attitude systems which are found to be fairly stable in most adults, and apparently the intention to learn is not necessary. Social rewards resulting from the acquisition of approved value-attitude systems play a big part in the process, especially when the system may be important to society but not beneficial to the individual. Linton (1947) cited courage in this connection, as a virtue inculcated in their members by most societies. It is necessary for the defence of the group, but cowardice may, in many circumstances, be more conducive to the self-preservation of individuals. In the short term, courage brings the reward of admiration, though in the long term it may result in the destruction of individuals.

The importance of any attitude depends on the importance of the object to which it refers. The attitude a child holds to itself is a vital factor in its development. Excessive self-love or self-hate does not make for healthy growth towards maturity, and children need to learn to see and accept themselves as they are and in relation to other people. They also need to learn a healthy attitude to authority, to be neither servile nor domineering but having a proper respect both for themselves and those individuals and institutions with which they come into contact.

Other important attitudes relate to the acceptance or rejection of members of other groups. These may be of people from outside the child's family or school, from another town or village or strangers from other countries or of other races. The future peace and happiness of the world may depend on the attitudes to outsiders of many types developed by children now at school.

Home, school and the wider society all have their part to play in the inculcation of attitudes and interests, and it will be part of the object of this book to study their influence. Another part will be concerned with a more detailed consideration of some important attitudes and interests. In particular, attitudes to self, to authority and to members of other groups will be studied. In this connection, those of us who are concerned with education need to know not only what attitudes we wish children to learn, but also what attitudes they already hold. One can travel successfully from A to B only if one has some idea where A and B both lie. In order to teach a child, we need to know his present state and to start from the point he has reached. Sometimes we might like to start somewhere else, but if we try to do so our teaching will not be effective. The ability to accept children as they really are, and not merely as they ideally might be, is essential for teachers, even though we must immediately proceed to make them more as we should like them to be. For this reason, a fairly detailed account will be given of investigations into the attitudes actually held by children and young people, as well as of ways in which they can be developed and modified.

For a fuller understanding of these topics, it will be necessary to include an account of the methods by which attitudes and interests can be assessed. These more technical chapters may also, it is hoped, be of help to those readers who wish to carry out inquiries of their own in this field.

II

ATTITUDES: DEVELOPMENT AND MODIFICATION

IT IS GENERALLY ACCEPTED that attitudes are learned and the widespread interest in the process bears witness to its importance in the modern world. Research in this field bears a marked resemblance to older work on social learning, and conditioning, suggestion and imitation are all involved. These appear to be the processes by which attitudes are inculcated in the first place or modified later, and knowledge of them is as useful to teachers as to propagandists. Both should be aware of the problem involved in deciding what attitudes are morally and socially desirable, as well as of the mechanics of developing them in young people. This is a subject about which great responsibility must be displayed, otherwise the result may be disastrous both for individuals and the community.

Most people are likely to acquire many of their attitudes in the homes in which they are brought up. A large part of the education of children consists in training and conditioning them to take their place in adult society, and parents provide examples which are constantly before their children. Parental attitudes, such as those towards the Church or towards foreigners, may be taken over by children and made their own, and this is one way in which their influence may be exerted. There is, however, another type of parental influence that must be considered.

Freudian theory teaches that the parents' behaviour and attitudes to the child are the primary elements in the environment in which he works out his adjustments, and there is plenty of evidence to support this. Shoben (1949) found a close connection between the behaviour of mothers and the adjustment of their children. Dominance, possessiveness and ignoring behaviour were far more marked among mothers of problem children than among mothers whose children did not show problem behaviour.

Dominance meant a tendency on the part of the mother to put the child in a subordinate role, to take full account of him, but as one who should conform to parental wishes or be severely punished. Possessiveness involved 'babying' the child and emphasising too strongly the affection between parent and child. Possessive mothers valued the dependence of their children and restricted their activities to those carried on in the family. At the opposite extreme were mothers who did not regard children as members of the family, but ignored them and saw as 'good' the child who made least demands on the parents' time. In this way, they disclaimed responsibility for their children's behaviour.

Over-protection and extreme rejection can both be disastrous for children, and Witmer (1937) found that delinquent, pre-psychotic, manic-depressive and schizophrenic children often had had to contend with adverse parental attitudes more than had normal children. In such cases, the success of psychiatric treatment may well depend on the attitudes of the parents. Sometimes maladjustment may be the result of the child's attempts to adapt to situations caused by parental attitudes.

Conflict at some stages between parents and children is not at all unusual, and the results are not always disastrous. Indeed, it is often found that as children become older they tend to adopt the attitudes of their parents in spite of earlier differences with them. This is sometimes the result of the development of a more mature outlook. If society is to be stable, some consistency of attitudes is required from generation to generation, and although changes do occur, and may seem great over a long period of time, the attitudes of consecutive generations on many issues are not very different. Bath and Lewis (1962), Glassey (1945) and Newcomb and Svehla (1937) all found

Attitudes: Development and Modification

similarities between the attitudes of parents and children towards such topics as the upbringing and education of children, religion and the Church, war, communism and sport.

Newcomb and Svehla (1937) noticed a closer relationship between the attitudes of parents and children at the lower end of the social scale. This may, perhaps, be because family life is often more closely knit in the lower classes than in higher ones. Children are less likely to be brought up by nurses and servants and so have closer contact with their mothers in formative years. Smaller houses may mean living together at closer quarters. As the children got older, there was a slight but consistent decline in the agreement between their attitudes and those of their parents, possibly reflecting the wider contacts they would be able to make as they became old enough to spend more time outside their homes.

Family resemblances in attitudes are probably not due solely to the personal influences of members on one another. They may also be due to the influence of institutions affecting all members, such as a Church to which they all belong, a school to which they all go, or the general environment in which they all live. Eysenck (1951b) found that in every political group he studied, the working class members were more toughminded than the middle class ones, and this was as true of the communists as of the conservatives. This would appear to be the result of the different kinds of environments in which they had been brought up and lived and which had helped to shape their outlooks.

Even when one has said that the attitude formed is a response to environmental conditions, it must be remembered that this response is the response of an individual. Individuals vary considerably in their natural endowments, physical, physiological and mental, and as a result the same response will not be possible nor desirable for everyone. For this reason, the attitudes formed by individuals are likely to be diverse, even though they are all subjected to very similar environmental conditions. Studies of the attitudes of different groups bring out the differences between groups, but even more marked, as a rule, is the range of attitudes within any one group. It is in this that we see the influence of genetic factors on the formation of attitudes.

Where the same family and the same environmental influences both act on children, they may be expected to result in more marked resemblances in attitude than where only one of these factors is at work. Brothers sent to the same school are likely to be more alike in outlook than if they went to different schools. Within a school population, Kulp and Davidson (1933) found closer similarities between the attitudes of siblings than between those of unrelated children to questions concerned with international, inter-racial, political and social problems. The correlations were comparable with those usually obtained between the intelligence test results of siblings and of unrelated children.

Although many attitudes are acquired during childhood as a result of home influences, these are not necessarily immutable. If they were, schools would have very little chance of doing anything more than teaching their pupils a certain amount of academic subject matter, and our concept of education would have to be changed. Fortunately, attitudes change and develop throughout life, and helping in this process is an important part of the work of teachers as well as of parents. It is important for anyone involved in educational work to know something of how attitudes can be modified, and this knowledge also throws light on the ways in which they can be inculcated. It is often easier to study a change of attitude than its original development.

A great many studies have been made of the changes that have occurred in the attitudes of students during their college courses. Students as a body are unusually available for testing as well as unusually amenable to it, and this probably accounts for the large number of experiments to which they have been subjected. This has prompted the comment that the study of attitudes has been largely the study of students' attitudes, and it is by no means certain that generalisations can be made from the results obtained with such a select population to the wider and much less select public. However this may be, it is very valuable for educationists to know as much as possible of the ways in which the attitudes of children and young people may be shaped.

Most studies of attitude changes have been carried out in the United States and it is not surprising to find that their authors were concerned with the liberalising of students' views and considered a shift from conservatism to radicalism as desirable. Often all that was done was to estimate the attitudes of students at the beginning, and again at the end, of a period in a particular college, the implication being that any change observed was due to the influence of the college. Studies of this type were made by Jones (1938), Lentz (1938) and Newcomb (1943 and 1947).

Changes of attitudes observed during college years were, as a rule, in the direction of greater liberalism. Students, coming up from a variety of homes and schools, usually had rather widely varying attitudes towards social, political and religious questions. At college, the student groups often tended to become more homogeneous in opinion, so that it was possible to speak of a typical attitude for a particular college.

Once established, this college attitude became the climate of opinion which new members encountered on entering college. Students entering a college like Bennington, described by Newcomb as very liberal in outlook, would find themselves members of a community greatly concerned over a wide range of public issues, unusually isolated and self-contained, and where both students and staff were very conscious of their membership of the college. Those from conservative homes would find an atmosphere like this more stimulating than would students who were already very liberal in their views, and it was found that these latter students were least affected by it. The more conservative students were the ones who changed most as a result of liberal college influences.

It was found, too, that there was a link between prestige and attitude. Students whose prestige was high were significantly less conservative than those whose prestige was low.

Here, again, the influence of the prevailing attitude in the college can be seen, approval being given to those who showed liberal rather than conservative attitudes and so conformed to the community picture of the good citizen.

Another factor investigated was amount of information about public issues. Among freshmen, no significant relationship was found, but among the same students in subsequent years the less conservative tended to be significantly better informed about public affairs than the more conservative.

In this case, Newcomb used a scale of attitude towards public affairs called *Political and Economic Progressivism (PEP)*, which was administered at intervals during the college course. In every year that this was done, it was found that the mean scores of the students showed decreasing conservatism from freshmen to seniors, and these differences were significant. Because no such changes were found at two neighbouring, but more conventional, colleges, it was concluded that the changes at Bennington were due to the more liberal outlook of the college.

This assumption does not seem to be entirely justifiable. To begin with, as Corey (1936) pointed out, the method of comparing group attitudes is not satisfactory. It is not sufficient to demonstrate differences between first, second and third year students at any one time unless there is evidence that, at the time of entry on the course, the attitudes of these groups were at least comparable. Nor is it sufficient to compare the mean scores of any one year group of students at different stages, since there is always a certain amount of wastage and change in the personnel of a group as it progresses through the course. If such a plan of experiment is to be used, then the average scores made by the students who complete the course must be compared with average scores of the same students at earlier stages, and not with average scores of the total group of which they were earlier a part. If this is not done, differences in group attitudes reported may be entirely caused by the defection of students whose attitudes did not agree with those of members who stayed the course. Corey produced evidence that there was, in the case he studied, a difference on entry between the original mean attitude of students who returned for the second and third years of the course and that of the whole group of which they were members on entry. Although the differences were small and not significant, they did indicate a trend, students returning for a second year being originally more liberal on average than the total group entering college, and those returning for a third year being more liberal still. In fact, it seemed that in this case the less liberal students had dropped out of the course.

What effect this might have had on the attitudes of those remaining can only be conjectured. The removal of the more conservative element could possibly be rather like the taking off of a brake, with consequent acceleration of change of attitude in the remainder in the liberal direction. Alternatively, the removal of opposition might result in stagnation. There is no indication of the true state of affairs.

Changes in the attitudes of students may be due to a variety of causes, only some of which are connected with their college or under its control. Authors of most of the studies mentioned have at least implied that they attached considerable importance to the general liberal atmosphere prevailing in the institutions concerned. The nature of the curriculum, the methods of presentation of subject matter, the social organisation and the outlook of the staff are frequently described as unusually liberal, while the students are, in some cases, pictured as coming from rather less liberal backgrounds. In many cases the college community is relatively self-contained, at least during term, and this situation is treated as being sufficiently controlled to ensure that where students show more liberal attitudes after a period of residence this can be claimed to be in great part due to the influence of the college. This assumption would require a good deal more justification than it has normally received.

Students have reached an age when they have sufficient knowledge to form opinions of their own and no longer need to take over those of their parents without criticism. They are more intelligent and more literate than the average member of the community, and so are able to read and evaluate a wide variety of opinions, not all of which are mediated through their college life unless this is more carefully supervised and organised for their indoctrination than is generally the case in free societies. The reaction of some young people against the opinions of their parents is not at all an unusual phenomenon in later adolescence. A recent survey among sixth form pupils in Britain showed around 40% as disagreeing with their parents' views on religion, politics and sex and well over 50% as disagreeing on aesthetics (*Sixth Form Opinion*, No. 4, June 20, 1962, pp. 19–25). Some of these pupils were in day schools, others were in boarding schools, but in either case it is unlikely that their opinions were shaped only by the school. Part of the process of growing up seems to be concerned with the formation of new attitudes or the modification of old ones, and this is likely to occur in all but the most confined circumstances.

Having said this, we must admit that there is some evidence that a suitably stimulating environment will provide an impetus to change of attitude. The desire to conform to the standards of an admired group is strong in most of us, and we do not take very much persuading to make us bring our own attitudes into line. This is what happens when students change the opinions they held at home for others more fashionable at the college of their choice. It happens in other contexts, too, and Scott and Brinkley (1960) provided an example of how the attitudes of student teachers towards their work could be improved by working in schools under teachers whose attitudes were superior to their own.

Another, but possibly related, method of inducing a change of attitude was discussed by Kelman (1962). He took the view that, if a person could be induced to act in some particular way, then there was a possibility that he would change his opinions so as to bring them into line with his actions. This resembles the process of rationalisation, whereby we often seek to justify something we have done by professing reasons which we claim to have had in mind before the action. When people are induced to take particular actions, where they can choose to do so or not, it may be that they are forced to reconsider their position, and this in turn may lead to a change of attitude.

Some earlier work by Kelman (1953) supports this view. Children, aged about 12, were asked their opinions about jungle stories and fantastic hero stories, and were found to favour the latter type. It was suggested that the former type was really the better, and they were asked to write essays on the subject. Some were told that they would get prizes if they wrote in favour of jungle stories, while others were given the chance to win prizes only if their essays were good enough. This group had to think out their reasons for stating a preference for jungle stories, and, because reward depended on the quality of their essays, they did so with some care. In doing so, they convinced themselves, and their attitudes changed far more in the direction of favouring jungle stories than did those of the group which was rewarded irrespective of the quality of their essays.

Similar results were obtained with army recruits by Myers (1921) and with older students by King and Janis (1956). Myers, working with men of low intelligence, simply taught them to write letters home in which they praised army conditions, but King and Janis, like Kelman, required students to supply reasoned arguments. Two different processes may be involved here, and it is possible that their relative effectiveness may depend on the intelligence of the subjects.

Bright individuals are more likely to have their opinions changed by conclusions based on factual information than are duller ones. They are more likely to be critical of the arguments used and are more sceptical, whereas duller people are more inclined to accept anything they are told. This was what happened with Myers's pupils. They were presented with statements about army life and they adopted them as their own views and repeated them in letters home. This is a much safer way of dealing with dull people than asking them to draw their own conclusions, since there is a fair chance that their reasoning may be faulty and they may draw the wrong conclusions.

Most people hold very tenaciously conclusions they themselves have drawn, whether the reasoning by which they have been reached is sound or not. Most teachers could produce illustrative examples. One class of grammar school girls asked repeatedly, as many others have done, 'Why should we learn mathematics?' The lesson was turned into a debate, with a chairman and speakers on both sides, the author, as teacher, being required to speak from the floor for and against the motion. Some of the arguments produced by the girls were startling in their irrelevance, but the class decided, overwhelmingly, that they ought to learn mathematics, and, more surprisingly, never raised the question again. They had convinced themselves.

The methods used in these enquiries bear a close resemblance to those employed by commercial advertisers. A company manufacturing soup is, at the time of writing, encouraging housewives to buy a wider range of its products than they usually do by paying half-a-crown for a specified set of labels from soup tins, some of which come from their less popular varieties. The idea is to get the public to try a wider range of soups, in the hope that they will continue to buy them. Other manufacturers are offering prizes ranging from foreign holidays to home movie sets for the best reasons for liking their goods, or for arranging their qualities in order of importance. Not only must the product be bought and tried, but the buyer must also think sympathetically about it. It is said that the results are very satisfactory to the manufacturers concerned in that they thus succeed in acquiring a greater share of the market. It is probably safe to assume that equally good results could be achieved by applying these methods to attitudes other than those towards soup.

Anyone wanting to use this method of swaying opinion should be very careful to see that the material used is foolproof. Even where there is no desire to coerce a group into forming a particular opinion, the use of material which is ambiguous may result in confusion. Apart from the possibility of faulty reasoning by some members, the facts presented may bear more than one interpretation. All this must be taken into account when using this method of influencing group attitudes. The simpler the material used, and the more direct the appeal, the more successful is it likely to be.

The importance of involving individuals personally in any scheme aiming at changing their attitudes is brought out by Lewin (1947a) and Bennett (1955). Lewin found group discussion a far more effective way of educating housewives in the use of particular foods than lecturing to them on the subject. Further work by Bennett suggested that other factors besides the method of presentation were involved. She considered that asking for a decision about future action increased the probability that it would be taken, whether this involved public commitment or not. A perceived consensus of opinion in a group also affected action, and discussion methods make it easier to see the trend of opinions of other members. The effect is to make waverers decide to conform with the majority decision, and this supports Lewin's (1947b) contention that it is easier to change the opinions of groups than of individuals.

A consideration of the results so far reviewed seems to indicate that the development or modification of an attitude depends on participation in the activities of groups already holding this attitude. This is what happens in the case of children. As members of their families they are surrounded by people subscribing to various opinions about what constitutes a desirable way of life. Whether they like it or not, children have to take part in the activities of their families, and in due course most of them develop attitudes resembling those of other members of their families. As the child's world widens, he is brought into contact with other groups, school, church, club, and so on, and by participation in their life he acquires their current attitudes. Some schools claim that their codes are caught rather than taught, but this is only a partial truth.

Attitudes: Development and Modification

These schools are often those which insist most strongly on conformity to their rules of behaviour, and in doing this they are in fact ensuring that the best possible conditions exist for 'catching' the attitudes responsible for the rules.

The methods by which conformity to the rules is ensured vary. In some institutions open insistence on obedience with penalties for failure to obey is used. In others the pressures are more subtle, and involve a demonstration of the factors contributing to prestige in the community. At Bennington, it was the individual holding liberal views who was admired, and students wishing for prestige were thus motivated to adopt liberal views. The atmosphere and the pressure to conform could not produce the desired attitude pattern unless this desire for approval and admiration were present. A student who despised the values of Bennington and did not wish to become an accepted member of the college community would have been unlikely to show a change of attitude in the direction of greater liberalism. It was noted that some individuals did not tend to adopt the prevailing views, but no definite case studies of these seem to have been made. It might be illuminating to consider what makes some pupils in all schools into noncomformists.

One point seems to be very clear. Simply to put children into a community holding definite attitudes with no inducement to conformity is unlikely to result in their adopting those attitudes as their own. It is more likely to result in their adopting no definite standard for themselves. Attitudes have to be learned, and an entirely permissive society omits to provide some of the factors which seem to be essential for successful learning. The fact of its permissiveness conveys the idea that no value is attached to any particular attitudes, and it also fails to ensure that children practice the behaviour which results from holding particular attitudes. Children are neither guided nor trained in such a society, and it is little wonder if the result is a generation of drifters. What can happen when such a generation is seized upon by an individual or organisation which demonstrates a definite attitude and imposes types of behaviour to correspond is not a matter for conjecture in this century. Those of us who were adults in 1939 remember only too well. None of us is likely to wish for another demonstration, and, that being so, we should consider carefully before we advocate too much permissiveness in the education of children.

Enforced conformity, however, does not of itself result in the adoption of current group attitudes. It is necessary also for conformity to bring rewards. These may be connected with increased prestige, as has been mentioned above, but they may also be connected with the discovery that the activity itself is enjoyable. Children compelled to learn a subject at school frequently find that they enjoy it and so develop a favourable attitude. What they enjoy may be some part of the subject matter, a method of working, something about a particular teacher, or the conditions under which the subject is studied.

Examples of ways in which enjoyment of work can change the attitudes of children are given by E. E. Evans (1962) and L. M. Brown (1959). By involving his pupils in the writing of verse, Evans succeeded in effecting a marked improvement in their attitude to poetry and in increasing their powers of literary discrimination. Brown adopted a method of group research in history, which his pupils enjoyed, and as they were led to see history as dealing with the lives of real people, so their attitudes to it improved.

Both these studies support the view that when enforced activity is found to be pleasurable it can result in the development of a more favourable attitude. The reverse is also likely to be true, but research aimed at making children's attitudes to school subjects less favourable is, understandably, lacking. Many children come to dislike some school subjects because of circumstances which have nothing to do with either the subject matter or their own ability, and when this happens it is wise to ask what extraneous factors are at work. The most probable cause of difficulty is likely to be connected with pupil-teacher relations.

17

Attitudes: Development and Modification

This chapter has attempted to show some of the ways in which attitudes can be developed and modified. This is essential knowledge for teachers, but they are not the only people seeking to affect the attitudes of others. We are constantly subjected to pressures from many sources, political, social and commercial, whose aims are to persuade or coerce us into particular kinds of behaviour. Sometimes this is for our own good, but often it is more for the benefit of the persuaders. Children growing up in this atmosphere should be made aware of what is going on and should learn to recognise the techniques being used to influence them. Concern has been expressed about the activities of some advertisers, and suggestions made for their restriction. A second line of defence is to make the public critical of advertisements and knowledgeable about the ways in which propagandists work. The education of a less suggestible and more thoughtful generation should be one of the aims of our schools and colleges. It will call for teachers who know clearly what they themselves are attempting and who do not accept too readily and without sufficient understanding either old or new purposes and ideals. The demands on them will be great, but the rewards for individuals and for society will be incalculable.

III

ATTITUDES: ASSESSMENT

TO OBTAIN A BETTER UNDERSTANDING of the findings of research on attitudes it is useful to know something of the ways in which they have been studied, so this chapter is devoted to a discussion of the methods commonly used. It is intended also as an introduction to the subject of attitude assessment for those readers who wish to carry out experiments themselves. It can be omitted or read later by those who do not, at this point, require the more technical information it contains.

The assessment of attitudes has, in recent years, been very widely attempted. The methods have varied from the sociological survey, which discovers the central tendency of a group but furnishes no information concerning its individual members, to psychophysical ones, which aim at assessing with considerable accuracy the relative attitudes of the individuals in the group. Indeed, the very variety of methods is of itself evidence, if this be needed, of the importance attached by psychologists and others to the attitudes displayed by individuals and groups.

One of the problems to be faced in assessing an attitude is that the very attempt at assessment may cause a change in the attitude. An individual, questioned about his attitude to, say, coloured peoples, may, for the first time in his life, bring his reason to bear on the subject. He has, until this point, behaved in relation to coloured people without thinking about his responses, but now he does think about them and he may decide to change his mode of behaviour. This end result may be all to the good, but the original attitude has been modified and can no longer be studied. Even when the change is not very marked, or does not occur at the level of conscious reasoning, the process of assessment is likely to result in a modification of the original attitude, and the realisation of this has affected some of the methods and techniques developed for attitude assessment.

Since an attitude is accompanied by a tendency to act in a particular way in given circumstances, it is sometimes possible to infer the attitudes of an individual from his behaviour. Most of us, however, are not in a position to make observations of this kind except to a very limited extent. It may sometimes be possible to set up an artificial experimental situation and watch the reactions of selected individuals placed therein, but this is cumbersome and time-consuming, and since the results have to be interpreted subjectively by the observer there is a large element of ambiguity involved. There is also no guarantee that the behaviour observed in the experimental situation will necessarily be paralleled in real life, and thus both the reliability and validity of the assessments are questionable. Neither controlled nor uncontrolled observation of behaviour is very satisfactory as a method of assessing attitudes.

A second method of assessment is based on a study of the expressed opinions of subjects. Opinion is often defined as the verbal expression of attitude, but if it is required to obtain an accurate assessment of attitude based on expressed opinions, safeguards are necessary. It is too easy for a subject, knowing that he is under observation, to formulate views more for the benefit of his examiner than because they are those which he himself holds. This may stem from the desire to oblige, the desire to show oneself in the most favourable light, the desire to shock, or some other motive of this type, quite as much as from a real dislike of displaying one's own true feelings. For this reason, disguised methods are often used when investigating attitudes, and the test may appear to be other than it really is. For example, a test of prejudice may be presented as a test of knowledge.

Another factor which affects the choice of method is the

use to which the information is to be put. Sometimes a single question will elicit all the information that is required. This is how parliamentary elections are conducted in this country at present, where the elector indicates which candidate, out of a list of two or more, he wishes to represent him in Parliament. There is no question of arranging the candidates in order of preference or of indicating how strongly he feels about the one for whom he votes. This is typical of the methods used in public opinion polls, whether they are concerned with politics, radio programmes or detergents.

A somewhat more sophisticated method employs an interview technique. The subject is encouraged to talk about himself and his views, and an assessment of his attitude is then made on the basis of what he says. Literate subjects may be asked to write a paragraph or so on the topic, and this can be taken away and analysed later. It is at least doubtful whether a written and a spoken statement would be assessed in quite the same way, even if they were identical in verbal content. The essay depends for its effect very much on the literary skill of the writer, but, even where this is high, can never convey the impressions of facial expression, voice and gesture gained during an interview. The use of tape-recordings might be supposed to obviate some of these difficulties, but it could not eliminate all of them, and none of these methods is particularly satisfactory. It is well known that neither interviews nor essays lend themselves to statistically reliable assessment, though careful training of interviewers and assessors can lead to improvement.

Projective techniques have in them something of both the controlled situation test and the interview or essay. The subject is faced with an ambiguous picture, such as those used in Murray's *Thematic Apperception Test*, and is asked to talk or write about it. His response is analysed by reference to norms based on the material supplied by large numbers of other subjects. This method has the advantage that the purpose of the test is not obvious, and the subject does not always realise the significance of what he says or writes. The test can be presented as a test of imagination, but the results can be analysed for indications of a particular attitude. Highly sophisticated subjects may spot the true purpose and refuse to co-operate, but in the main the test arouses interest and is often considered to be pleasurable. Like the interview and essay, the projection test response has to be analysed subjectively and an element of unreliability is thus introduced.

An appreciation of the need for more objective means of assessing attitudes has led to the development of various types of attitude scales. The usual form consists of a set of statements with which agreement or disagreement can be expressed, and the resulting scores distribute the test population along the attitude continuum. The usefulness of the scale will depend very much on the skill with which the statements of which it is composed are selected and combined, and much effort has been expended on the refinement of techniques of scale construction.

In his pioneer work in this connection, Thurstone (1927 and 1959) attempted to employ the method used in investigating the ability of individuals to perceive small differences in, for example, weights. Instead of weights, he used pairs of statements and asked the subjects to classify them as more or less favourable, and he reasoned that the linear difference between two statements was equivalent to the percentage of judges who could perceive the difference. The method is, however, too cumbersome for use with large numbers of statements. In general, if there are n statements, the number of paired comparisons is $n(n-1)/2$, and if $n = 20$, this gives 190 pairs.

A similar, but less laborious, method of scaling statements was devised by Thurstone and Chave (1929). They compiled a list of 130 statements and submitted them to a group of 300 judges, with a request that they should be divided into eleven piles, ranging from very, very unfavourable statements to very, very favourable ones. The piles were then numbered from one to eleven, and the frequencies with which any particular statement was allotted to the piles were noted. A cumulative frequency graph was drawn, and from it the median value assigned to the statement was obtained. This was taken as the scale value of the attitude of those who expressed agreement with that statement. In order to decide whether the statement did, in fact, denote a definite attitude, the interquartile range was also found from the graph. If this was large, the statement was assumed to be ambiguous and likely to be endorsed by people holding very different opinions. Such statements were discarded in drawing up the final form of the test.

For the final form, 45 of the original statements were selected, giving a more or less evenly graduated series of values throughout the whole range of the scale. The test was then given to a group of subjects, who were asked to check the statements with which they agreed. The mean scale value of statements checked by an individual was taken as a measure of his attitude.

Examples of the scaling of attitude statements by the Thurstone and Chave method are given in the appendix at the end of this chapter.

A practical modification of the Thurstone technique was devised by Remmers (1954). This consisted of general scales, which referred not to individual objects but to classes or groups of objects. Thus one general scale could be used to measure attitude to a given national group simply by inserting the required designation in a set of attitude statements which could refer to any national group. Other scales could assess attitudes to any social institution, vocation, school subject, teacher, and so on. In this way, a few scales could be used to assess a very large number of attitudes. Vernon (1953) has expressed doubts about the value of these general scales.

Another method of constructing and scoring an attitude scale, due to Likert (1932) and also described by Likert, Roslow and Murphy (1934), dispensed with the group of judges required by the Thurstone and Chave technique. Here the attitude questionnaire consisted of a set of equal numbers of favourable and unfavourable statements with which each

23

subject was directed to indicate the extent of his agreement
in the following manner.

If you agree with a statement, put a plus. $(+)$

If you agree strongly with a statement, put a plus with
a circle round it. $(\oplus)$

If you disgree with a statement, put a minus. $(-)$

If you disagree strongly with a statement, put a minus
with a circle round it. $(\ominus)$

If you are undecided, put a question mark. $(?)$

To obtain the subject's score on the scale, one extreme of
the attitude continuum was designated as numerically high and
this extreme alternative was given a value 5. The other extreme
was given a value 1. The question mark was scored 3. As a
rule the favourable end was scored 5. With unfavourable statements these values were reversed and strong agreement was
scored 1, while strong disagreement was scored 5; the value
of the question marked remained at 3. Intermediate positions
scored 2 and 4. The final score was the sum of the numbers
corresponding to the opinions expressed.

In order to decide whether the numerical values had been
assigned consistently, the highest and lowest scoring 25% of
the group of subjects were taken and their responses to each
statement were tabulated. If the values were correctly assigned,
the sum of the responses of the high group should be higher
than that for the low group for each statement. If, on any
statement, the high group scored lower than the low group,
the alternatives had been reversed during scoring.

Where the two groups produced similar aggregate scores,
the statement in question had failed to discriminate and was
unsuitable. In general, this was found to be true of statements
which fell near the middle of the Thurstone scale, and only
statements expressing definitely favourable or unfavourable
attitudes could be used. Double-barrelled statements were also
unsuitable, as it was sometimes possible to agree with one part
and disagree with the other, so that agreement with the same
statements might be expressed by people with widely differing

Attitudes: Development and Modification

attitudes. This method of attitude assessment was claimed to be consistently more reliable than the Thurstone and Chave method, and a survey by Edwards (1957) of the evidence from a number of studies bore this out.

An alternative but equivalent method of scoring has been used by Fleming in the *Cotswold Personality Assessment (P.A.* 1). In this test, the subjects were asked to arrange their responses in two columns, those to the favourable statements in the left hand column and those to the unfavourable ones on the right. These columns were summed separately, and the excess of favourable over unfavourable votes gave the final attitude score. Because of the necessity for avoiding neutral statements, some investigators have used the Thurstone-Chave method of scaling, choosing for the test only those statements which the judges rank at the extremes of the scale. Scoring is then by some version of the Likert method. Fleming's test, already mentioned, is one example of this, and another is the author's own test *Teachers and Teaching* (Evans, 1946) whose construction is described in the appendix to this chapter.

An important part of the construction of an attitude scale is the collection of the statements from which the scale will be composed. If it can be ensured that only statements which are likely to be suitable are submitted to the judges for rating, much unnecessary work can be eliminated. For this reason, it is worth taking a good deal of trouble over drawing up the original list. A useful set of informal criteria for attitude statements has been compiled by Edwards (1957) after reference to earlier investigations.

In the first place, care should be taken that the statements collected are relevant to the attitude under consideration, and that they are statements of opinion and not of fact. A statement which is merely right or wrong, true or untrue, will be accepted or rejected by all, or almost all, and will not help to sort out according to attitude those for whom the test is designed.

It is always important to keep the test population in mind, and to couch the statements in language which they are likely to understand. Simple, clear statements, which are not too long and which avoid double negatives and words like *all*, *never*, *only* and *merely* are best. Double-barrelled statements may introduce ambiguity, and should not be used for that reason. It is true that both irrelevance and ambiguity are likely to come to light in the process of scaling, but it is unnecessary to start with unsuitable statements in order to discard them. For teaching purposes, it may sometimes be useful to ask a group to try to scale an ambiguous or irrelevant statement, but serious research workers want to obtain the best possible results by the most economical method.

Another factor which appears to have some effect on attitude scores is the acceptability of the form of the statements, as Rundquist (1940) found in the case of the children he tested. It is easy to understand why, if a subject finds a statement offensive, he may react emotionally and, in an extreme case, refuse to co-operate. The success of an experiment may well depend on the courtesy with which the subjects are treated, and this should be remembered when deciding on the form of statements to be included in an attitude scale.

It is sometimes asked whether the personal attitudes of the judges of the original statements have any effect on the way they scale them. Hinckley (1932) and Pintner and Forlano (1937) attacked this problem in quite distinct ways, and both found that the opinions held by the judges did not warp their intellectual judgment of the meaning of attitude statements. Judges were able to put themselves in the place of another person and assess objectively the meaning, to him, of a particular statement irrespective of whether they themselves agreed with it or not.

Doubts are sometimes expressed about the truthfulness of the answers given on personality and attitude scales. It is argued that most people, whether intentionally or not, tend to falsify their responses, saying what they think is most flattering to themselves, rather than giving their real opinions. Spencer (1938) conducted an enquiry into the frankness of high school pupils on a test which they thought was anonymous, and concluded that about 55% might have been expected to answer without deliberate falsification.

Signed and unsigned questionnaires may sometimes be filled in differently, but this is not always the case, as Corey (1937a) found. Such factors as the use to which people think their answers may be put and the relationship between them and the investigator may have a marked effect on the answers in some circumstances. Students will nearly always co-operate in a piece of research, as long as they know that there will be no repercussions for them personally. When the author asked students to fill in the *Minnesota Teacher Attitude Inventory* twice, the first time honestly and the second time with a view to creating the best possible impressions of themselves, the difference between the two sets of scores was very marked. Under these conditions, they had definitely answered truthfully on the first occasion, but they might not have done so if their examination results or future careers had depended on the results. The second set of scores demonstrated that they knew very well how to create a good impression of themselves if they so wished. (Evans, 1958.)

A different, and probably more important, question is concerned with the extent to which attitudes as indicated by scales correlate with actual behaviour, and a good deal of work has been done on this. The whole question of the validity of attitude scales is involved here.

McNemar (1946) listed five ways of establishing the validity of an attitude scale. In the first, the attitude as denoted by the test score is compared with observable behaviour in a corresponding situation, and the extent to which they agree is taken as a measure of the validity of the scale. When Corey (1937b) used this method, he found little relationship between students' opinions about honesty and the extent to which they cheated on tests. This latter seemed to be more closely related to the amount of preparation they had done and the ease of the tests. On easy tests, cheating was unnecessary whatever views the students held about it. On difficult ones, even the most honest might be tempted.

Other enquiries, with different types of subjects, have produced similar results. Pace (1950) found that people who held opinions strongly were likely to act in accordance with them, whether it was sensible to do so or not. Less committed people tended to be less calculable in their behaviour. Zunich (1962) observed the behaviour of mothers towards their small children and found that it bore little relation to their scores on a test of attitude to children.

In cases such as these, attitude scales do not appear to be very good predictors of behaviour. It must always be remembered, though, that the estimation of behaviour is subjective and may itself be an unsatisfactory criterion, judged statistically. Where the criterion is more objective, better results are obtained. Adams (1962) found considerable agreement between the attitudes of students to the subjects of the curriculum and their choices of optional subjects. Here the reliability of the attitude scales used was high and the choice of subjects could be observed accurately, so that subjectivity was at a minimum.

Both Adams and Corey (1937b) realised that other factors besides opinion affect behaviour, and it is necessary to take these into account if an accurate estimate of the connection between attitude and behaviour is required. A student may choose to study a disliked subject if it is necessary for entry to a much desired career. Expensive hobbies, no matter how attractive, cannot be followed where money is lacking. Considerations of family duty may deter some from taking up work which would otherwise be chosen. Opinions and attitudes are often quite sincerely held, even though they are not matched by observable behaviour.

McNemar's second method of estimating validity involves consideration of the extent to which the scale differentiates the members of groups whose opinions are known. Thurstone and Chave used this method to obtain evidence of the validity of their scale of attitude towards the Church and found that it differentiated between Divinity students and others, between students of various religious affiliations, and between active Church members and those with less interest in Church affairs.

Eysenck, too, used this method to validate his *Inventory of Social Attitudes*, showing that groups whose political affiliations were known could be differentiated by it. The author's own test, *Teachers and Teaching*, described in the appendix to this chapter, was found to discriminate between Sixth Form girls who wished to teach and those who did not.

Scores for different groups on any test of this kind are likely to overlap, even if differences between their means are in the direction one would expect. Nevertheless, when scales do not give absurd results with groups whose attitudes are known, it is not unreasonable to use them for investigating the opinions of groups whose attitudes are not known.

The third method of validation mentioned by McNemar involves correlation of test scores with ratings of attitudes made by close acquaintances of the subjects. Added to the inaccuracies likely to result from the use of subjective ratings of this kind, there is another source of error here due to the fact that the ratings will not all have been made by the same person. This method seems to introduce altogether too many sources of error to be very useful.

The fourth method involves checking against a known scale. If a scale of satisfactory validity already exists, there seems little point in preparing another, but if this is required the method is sound enough. The difficulty is likely to be to find one existing well-validated scale.

The last method involves interviewing the subjects to see whether, when catechised about their opinions, they stand up to cross-examination. This method, again, introduces a large subjective element. A modification was used by Thurstone and Chave (1929) when they obtained self-ratings of attitude to the Church from their subjects. Using a graphic rating scale, they obtained self-ratings which correlated to an extent of $+0.67$ with scores on the attitude scale. They considered this fairly satisfactory, but they refused to draw any significant inferences from it because of their lack of knowledge of the reliability of the self-ratings.

It should be obvious by now that it is not easy to validate

an attitude scale. Neither is it easy to get an estimate of reliability. Attitudes are subject to change, and a low test-retest correlation may mean either that the scale is unreliable or that fluctuations of attitude have occurred during the interval between tests. If this interval is too short for changes to have occurred, the retest may measure memory as much as attitude.

Adams (1962) asked students filling in an attitude questionnaire for the second time after an interval of eight months to indicate any change they believed had taken place in their attitudes and also how sure they were that they recalled their former attitudes correctly. While students who indicated a change of attitude usually proved to be correct in judging its direction, only a minority recalled their original scores accurately. The test-retest reliability for the whole sample of 190 students was $+0.78$, and for those (134) who thought their attitudes had not changed it was $+0.83$. In this case, the influence of recall of earlier results was considered to be very small, but eight months is a fairly long interval and it would not be safe to assume that the same would be true if a shorter time had elapsed between tests.

A split-half technique can be used with tests which split easily into equivalent halves. If this method is to be used, it should be kept in mind when choosing the attitude statements, so that the test can be divided up accurately. As an alternative, two versions of the test can be constructed and their reliabilities checked by intercorrelating scores on them from the same group. Thurstone and Chave used a split-half technique with their scale of attitude towards the Church, and obtained a reliability coefficient of $+0.848$, which was raised by the Spearman-Brown formula to $+0.92$ for the whole test. Frenkel-Brunswik (1948) obtained uncorrected split-half reliabilities of between $+0.82$ and $+0.90$ for her tests of ethnic prejudice, and Adams (1962) obtained one of $+0.89$ using a Likert type test, and of $+0.71$ using equivalent forms of a Thurstone and Chave test.

According to Vernon (1938), most attitude tests have quite

high reliability, often between $+0.75$ and $+0.90$, and this is borne out by the figures just quoted. The more varied the items included in a scale, the greater is likely to be its reliability, for variations in opinions about individual items are more likely to cancel out in this case than when the items are all very similar. The reliability of a test will also depend on the heterogeneity of opinions expressed by the individuals being tested, for the greater the range of scores obtained the higher will be the correlation between sets of scores obtained on different occasions. Vernon (1938) considered it undesirable to aim at too high a reliability in devising an attitude test, because if the items are too homogeneous it becomes very easy for the subject to present his own picture of himself rather than his true opinions. In other words, validity may be sacrificed to reliability.

Allied to the problems of validity and reliability, is the problem of ensuring that all the items of a scale do, in fact, refer to the same attitude continuum. Thurstone and Chave's use of judges in determining scale values gives help here, for the judges' ratings will disclose any ambiguity or irrelevancy in the statements, and the final selection of items is likely to have considerable internal consistency. Another approach to the problem of unidimensionality has been described by Guttman (1950).

Guttman starts from the necessity of ensuring that there is an order in which the attitudes of individuals can be arranged between two points, and the comment by Murphy, Murphy and Newcomb (1937) that a scale is not really a scale unless one can tell that an individual holding a given attitude will also hold all those to one side of it and none of those to the other side. Murphy, Murphy and Newcomb did not think such rigorous scaling of social attitudes possible, but Guttman (1950) claimed that it is. His technique of scalogram analysis depends on the ranking of individuals, not the ranking of items, and a consideration of the items endorsed by individuals.

A few attitude statements which are relatively homogeneous in content are selected and given to a sample of about a hundred

31

persons, who are asked to respond either with *agree* or *disagree*. These responses are weighted *1* or *0*, and a score is obtained for each subject. Individual scores are then arranged in order from high to low, and the responses of each subject to each statement are tabulated. If the statements conform to Guttman's requirements, then, for any item, those subjects who score *1* for it should rank above those who score *0* for it, and this should be true for every item. With a perfect scale, knowledge of an individual's score would make possible reproduction of the complete pattern of his responses, but this degree of perfection is rarely achieved. The process is laborious, and Guttman's (1941) original method of scaling is no longer employed, having been replaced by his Cornell technique. (Guttman, 1947, 1950.) Scalogram analysis has also been used in other contexts, such as the study of children's perception and thinking. (Peel, 1959.)

The disadvantage of the method is that the attitude statements used have to be relatively homogeneous in content, and, as a result, the attitude under investigation has to be narrowly defined. Instead of investigating attitude to teaching as a career and considering many aspects of the topic as is done in the test *Teachers and Teaching*, it would be necessary to consider aspects separately, dealing with attitudes to the work in the classroom, to the social status of teachers, to teachers' salaries, and to the social usefulness of the career as separate scales.

Another serious difficulty encountered in attitude scaling is concerned with the units of the scale. To permit of free arithmetical manipulation, these units need to be equal, and the assumption is made that the units obtained by whatever scaling technique is employed are equal. This is a very doubtful assumption, and McNemar (1946) was probably right when he stated that, while it is possible to secure a reliable and valid rank order of individuals along a single attitude continuum, no method exists which will give units which are really equal.

Fuller discussions of the requirements of a satisfactory attitude scale will be found in the work of Droba (1932) and

Ferguson (1937b). The indirect assessment of social attitudes has been discussed at some length by Campbell (1950).

Because of the difficulties involved in constructing satisfactory attitude tests of the types already discussed, a new approach was tried by Cattell, Maxwell, Light and Unger (1949). This depended on what they called psychodynamic methods, and they tested such variables as time and money expenditure, immediate memory, psychogalvanic reflex response and changes in pulse pressure as indicators of attitudes. The results, looked at dispassionately, did not appear particularly satisfactory, though their authors suggested that they might be made more so by technical improvements. Tests of this kind might, of course, be more fun, both for experimenter and subjects, than ordinary attitude scales.

Although important work has been done on the assessment of attitudes, there is considerable scope still for improvements in the methods used. The field has attracted many workers and there is no reason to suppose that its fascination is diminishing. As long as the need remains to explain human behaviour, so long are attempts to study and assess attitudes likely to continue.

APPENDIX: AN EXAMPLE OF THE CONSTRUCTION OF AN ATTITUDE SCALE

Some years ago, the author undertook a study of the attitudes towards teaching as a career of grammar school pupils aged about sixteen. It was obvious, then as now, that a great many extra teachers were going to be needed and, because most of them would have to come from among the pupils in the grammar schools, the opinions of those pupils on this subject were important. As part of this work, an attitude scale was drawn up, using the Thurstone and Chave technique for scaling statements. An account of the construction of this scale follows, to illustrate the method more fully.

First a list of sixty-three statements was compiled, covering such aspects of the career as the nature and conditions of work, the training, status and salaries of teachers, their personal qualities and relationships with their colleagues and with the general public. Examples of the statements used are:

(9) Teachers are usually very unselfish.

(17) Teaching would be dull as teachers only deal with facts out of books.

(21) There are few chances of promotion for teachers.

(40) One attraction of teaching is that there are plenty of grants and scholarships available for people who want to become teachers.

(42) The training for teaching gives one the opportunity to learn a great many interesting things.

(46) Teachers are respected by other people.

(53) I should like to be a teacher as well as anything else.

(56) Teachers have the opportunity to do a great deal of good.

(62) Teaching would be interesting because it would mean dealing with children.

The whole list was sent to a group of experienced judges with the following instructions:

'Each of the statements on the enclosed sheet is concerned with teaching or teachers. Read the first statement and decide whether the person who made it is likely to be considering in a favourable or unfavourable way the possibility of taking up teaching as a career.

If you decide that they are considering it favourably, mark that statement A; if unfavourably, mark it C; if you cannot tell, mark it B. Then consider all the other statements in the same way.

Now go through the statements marked A and decide on the degree of favourableness they show. Mark them as follows:

      A1   very, very favourable.
      A2   very favourable.
      A3   favourable.

Continue with the B and C statements.

      B1   slightly favourable.
      B2   strictly neutral.
      B3   slightly unfavourable.
      C1   unfavourable.
      C2   very unfavourable.
      C3   very, very unfavourable.

It does not matter whether you yourself agree or disagree with the statements. They have been made by different people and the object is to discover the opinions of these people about teaching as a career.'

When the lists were returned, the classifications were converted into numerical ratings from 9 for A1 to 1 for C3. Some of the lists had to be discarded as the instructions had not been followed correctly, but forty remained in which the rating appeared to have been completed satisfactorily. These lists were then analysed and a table showing the frequencies of the ratings given to each statement was drawn up. From this table, another table showing the cumulative frequencies was prepared and the result for each statement was graphed. From the graphs, the median and quartile ratings of each statement were read off and the interquartile ranges were calculated. Extracts from these tables follow, and an example of one of the graphs.

TABLE 1.
FREQUENCIES OF RATINGS BY JUDGES

Statement	Frequencies of ratings								
	1	2	3	4	5	6	7	8	9
9	0	0	0	0	3	7	10	14	6
17	13	18	5	2	1	0	1	0	0
21	7	7	19	6	1	0	0	0	0
40	1	0	0	0	3	7	10	16	3
42	0	0	0	0	0	1	6	19	14
46	0	1	0	1	1	12	9	10	6
53	0	0	1	3	16	10	5	3	2
56	0	0	0	0	2	3	6	17	12
62	0	0	0	0	0	2	4	21	13

TABLE 2.
CUMULATIVE FREQUENCIES OF RATINGS BY JUDGES

Statement	Cumulative frequencies of ratings								
	1	2	3	4	5	6	7	8	9
9	0	0	0	0	3	10	20	34	40
17	13	31	36	38	39	39	40	40	40
21	7	14	33	39	40	40	40	40	40
40	1	1	1	1	4	11	21	37	40
42	0	0	0	0	0	1	7	26	40
46	0	1	1	2	3	15	24	34	40
53	0	0	1	4	20	30	35	38	40
56	0	0	0	0	2	5	11	28	40
62	0	0	0	0	0	2	6	27	40

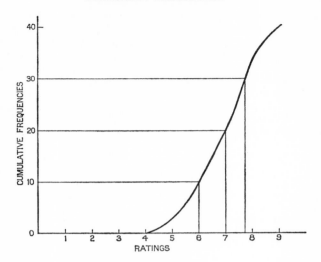

GRAPH OF CUMULATIVE FREQUENCIES OF RATINGS
FOR STATEMENT 9.

TABLE 3.

MEDIAN AND QUARTILE RATINGS

Statement	Median	Quartiles		Interquartile Range
9	7·0	6·0	7·7	1·7
17	1·4	0·9	1·9	1·0
21	2·4	1·6	2·8	1·2
40	6·9	5·9	7·6	1·7
42	7·7	7·2	8·2	1·0
46	6·6	5·7	7·7	2·0
53	5·0	4·5	6·0	1·5
56	7·7	6·8	8·1	1·3
62	7·9	7·5	8·2	0·7

Attitudes: Assessment

When all the information was available, a set of statements was chosen which covered all aspects of the subject, whose median ratings were low or high, and the interquartile ranges of whose ratings were small. This ensured that the test was suitable for scoring by a modified Likert technique, and that the items in it were not ambiguous. In a few cases, rewording was necessary to remove possible ambiguities. For each statement, there was included another which expressed an approximately equal and opposite attitude, so that the expression of all shades of opinion was possible within the scope of the test. Instructions to the subjects were added as shown in the complete test which follows. Votes in the left-hand column, applying to favourable statements, were counted as positive, those in the right-hand column as negative, since they applied to unfavourable statements. The final score was the difference between the sums of the votes in the two columns. The range of possible scores was from $+48$ to -48.

TEACHERS AND TEACHING

Some boys and girls were talking about teachers and teaching. Here are some of the things they said. Give 4 votes to each statement with which you agree very strongly, 3 to those with which you are inclined to agree, 2 to those about which you are doubtful, 1 to those with which you are inclined to disagree and 0 to those with which you disagree very strongly. Put your votes on the heavy lines besides the statements.

1. Only people who can do nothing else become teachers.
2. Teaching would not be monotonous.
3. Teachers lead very narrow lives.
4. There are plenty of good jobs for teachers.
5. Too much of a teacher's work has to be done indoors.
6. Teaching is an important form of social service.
7. There are few chances of promotion for teachers.
8. Teachers are well paid.
9. The short hours of the school day make teaching attractive.
10. No one would be any worse off if there were never any more teachers.

11. Teaching is not sufficiently well paid to be an attractive profession.　· · · ·　· · · ·　——

12. Teaching is a safe job with a pension at the end.　——　· · · ·　· · · ·

13. There are plenty of grants and scholarships available for people who want to become teachers.　——　· · · ·　· · · ·

14. Training as a teacher gives an opportunity to learn a great many interesting things.　——　· · · ·　· · · ·

15. Teaching is interesting because it involves meeting many people.　——　· · · ·　· · · ·

16. Nothing would ever persuade me to become a teacher.　· · · ·　· · · ·　——

17. Training as a teacher is too narrow to be interesting.　· · · ·　· · · ·　——

18. Teaching is interesting because it means dealing with children.　——　· · · ·　· · · ·

19. I am determined to become a teacher.　——　· · · ·　· · · ·

20. Teaching is dull because teachers deal only with facts out of books.　· · · ·　· · · ·　——

21. Teaching is not sufficiently well paid to make its expensive training worth while.　· · · ·　· · · ·　——

22. Many people would like to be teachers if they could.　——　· · · ·　· · · ·

23. Teaching is monotonous work.　· · · ·　· · · ·　——

24. Teaching must be a very unpleasant job when one gets old.　· · · ·　· · · ·　——

For full details of the construction of this test, see Evans (1946).

IV

ATTITUDES: ORGANISATION

THE DEVELOPMENT OF METHODS of attitude assessment at more or less the time when factor analytical techniques were being intensively studied resulted in a number of attempts at discovering basic attitude factors. An early lead in this work was given by Thurstone (1934), who described an experiment in which T. G. Thurstone factor analysed the results of a large number of attitude scales given to university students. She obtained a conspicuous common factor, which she recognised as radicalism, and a second, less well-defined factor, which was tentatively called nationalism. Further work by Ferguson (1939a, 1940) also produced evidence of two factors, but Ferguson preferred to describe them as religionism and humanitarianism.

More recently, Eysenck and his followers have taken up this work with enthusiasm and have attempted to identify and measure a few attitudes, themselves unrelated but to which other attitudes are related. They postulate a hierarchical system, organised on four different levels. At the lowest level are to be found opinions, expressed on the spur of the moment in specific situations to which they are reactions. They may never be repeated and little importance can be attached to most of them.

At the next level are to be found habitual opinions, held in respect of subjects or situations which are stable or recurring. They are likely to be expressed repeatedly, in more or less the same form, on suitable occasions or in response to particular stimuli. Where a number of these opinions relate to the same topic, they become associated together at a higher level as indicators of a true attitude. Ethnocentrism is cited by Eysenck (1953b, 1954) as such an attitude, whose existence is indicated by habitual opinions expressed about people of many other nationalities.

At the highest level are to be found what Eysenck termed ideologies, compounded of a number of related attitudes. As such an ideology he cited conservatism, compounded of related attitudes such as ethnocentrism, patriotism, pro-religious attitudes and attitudes concerned with the strict upbringing of children.

This theory is based upon an examination of a large amount of earlier work, published by other investigators, and the factor analysis of data obtained by using attitude questionnaires. The first ideology or type-level attitude to emerge from these researches was one labelled radicalism-conservatism and usually referred to as R. The second factor found was labelled by Eysenck (1953b, 1954), following William James (1925), tendermindedness-toughmindedness, and he referred to it as T.

As a result of his investigations, Eysenck drew up an *Inventory of Social Attitudes* composed of items shown to be of importance in previous researches. When it was administered to a selected group of adult students, the results were checked satisfactorily against their known political affiliations.

To the factors R and T, George (1954) added a third, labelled neuroticism, and a fourth, independent of R and neuroticism but not of T, which appeared to correspond to extraversion-introversion. Eysenck himself (1954), suggested that T might not be an ideological system like R, but might be more concerned with a set of personality variables affecting social attitudes. Support for this idea came from Melvin (1955), who regarded it as probable that T might correspond to introversion-extraversion as described by Jung (1923). More recently, however, Carrigan (1960) has shown grounds for doubting whether introversion-extraversion is really an independent dimension of personality.

Like Jung, Spranger (1928) attempted to classify people in

terms of their evaluative attitudes or values, and though he might be considered to be thinking in terms of interest rather than of attitudes, his work is mentioned here because of the use which has been made of it in the study of social attitudes. Basing his classification on philosophical considerations, Spranger postulated that people showed more or less consistent and permanent attitudes or sets, and that six ideal types of individuality could be discriminated. These he called theoretical, economic, aesthetic, social, political and religious, and he allowed that, in real life, any particular person might not belong exclusively to any one type, but might show characteristics of more than one.

Spranger's classification was based on reasoning, not on experiment, but this reasoning appeared to be of a type which could be tested empirically, and an attempt to do this was made by Allport and Vernon (1931), using a questionnaire which they entitled *A Study of Values*. Revisions of this test have been published by Allport, Vernon and Lindzey in 1951 and 1960. It is designed for college students or adults of a similar educational level.

The *Study of Values* is a well-standardised test, and good reliability and validity coefficients have been reported for it. The importance attached to it can be judged from the reviews of work in which it has been used, published by Duffy in 1940 and Dukes in 1955. Not all tests have as long a life as this, and the fact that the *Study of Values* has survived for thirty years, during which time a major World War with the consequent disruption of society has occurred, suggests that it is not dealing merely with superficial levels of personality organisation. This being so, findings based on its use deserve serious consideration.

After reviewing a large number of investigations, Duffy (1940) reported that the findings indicated that among students the value scores obtained are fairly constant during the college years, but that there is a tendency for theoretical and aesthetic, and possibly also social, values to increase. This could be taken as evidence that values or evaluative attitudes are learned, not inborn, or at least are modifiable according to the circumstances in which the individual finds himself. It is not surprising that students, during the years in which they are deeply immersed in intellectual pursuits and exposed to the influence of ideas to an extent which is uncommon in most walks of life, should change their values in the directions indicated. Duffy showed that there are grounds for believing that evaluative attitudes, however they come into being, are pervasive and enduring and can be regarded as generalised traits of personality.

Whether the evaluative attitudes which Spranger suggested as basic are really independent is a different question, and one which the factor analysts have attempted to answer. Lurie (1937) suggested four basic clusters of attitudes.

1. Social, typical of the person who values especially human relations.
2. Philistine, corresponding to the emphasis of utility and power at the expense of beauty and harmony.
3. Theoretical, stress being laid on truth and cognitive values.
4. Religious, having a particular regard for the spiritual side of life.

Three less important factors were described as open-mindedness, practicality, and an aesthetic attitude of a superficial and onlooking rather than a participating sort.

Lurie believed that a more self-consistent system of personality classification could be built upon his four main types than upon Spranger's original six, and, judging from Duffy's report (1940), it seems likely that some such reduction is possible. According to this, all investigators have found that theoretical and social values are positive and distinct attitudes. There are doubts whether this is true of economic and political values, and it is possible that aesthetic values may be neither positive nor distinct, but rather anti-economic and political with a tendency to be pro-theoretical. In the same way it has been suggested that religious values may be considered to be a lack of interest in economic, political and theoretical values.

As a result of a study of the relations between personal

values, social attitudes and personality traits, George (1954) concluded that values and attitudes are not entirely independent of one another, but have some kind of pattern or organisation. Considering the factor radicalism-conservatism, he found that political, economic and religious values appeared to be associated with the conservative end of the continuum, while theoretical, aesthetic and social values were to be found at the radical end. At the same time, economic, political and theoretical values appeared at the toughminded end of another continuum, opposed to religious, aesthetic and social values at the tenderminded end. Analysis of variance, taking into account known political affiliations, showed that conservatives were more economic and religious, while radicals were more social, aesthetic and theoretical in their value systems.

The connection between values and attitudes does seem to be fairly well established. Indeed, Linton (1947) linked the definitions of the two terms. He considered *value* to be a common element in a series of situations, which can evoke a covert response in an individual, and that this covert response is an attitude. Taken together, the value and the attitude constitute a stimulus-response situation, which may be called a value-attitude system. Systems of this kind, he held, operate automatically and often below the level of consciousness, and one system may provide the motivations for a number of different behaviour patterns. Linton cited cruelty as such a value-attitude system, which may in some circumstances lead an individual to interfere and in others to withdraw and do nothing.

Theories of the basic nature of attitude factors, when these rest on findings from studies carried out only in areas of Europe and the United States where very similar cultures prevail, are open to criticism. Keehn (1955) questioned Eysenck's theory of the universality of the radicalism-conservatism factor, and held that this merely reflected the current political ideology of Britain and other Western countries. To test this hypothesis, he had Eysenck's inventory filled out by students at the American University of Beirut in the Lebanon, after modifying it slightly so as to eliminate some minor linguistic difficulties.

In this Near-Eastern culture, radicalism-conservatism is not the major political issue, and analysis of the inter-item correlations produced a first factor different from that obtained by Eysenck. It was, in fact, identified as Arab Nationalism. Keehn argued that Eysenck had presented a special case of a more general attitude pattern, and that the first factor obtained is likely to be related to the major political issue of the culture under investigation. In Britain this would be radicalism, while in the Lebanon it would be Arab Nationalism.

Eysenck's second factor of toughmindedness-tendermindedness was assumed by Keehn to be a true personality dimension and related to introversion-extraversion, and his analysis established the existence of a second factor of this type, independent of the first. Support for this idea is forthcoming from a recent piece of work by Digman (1962).

Most of the studies so far considered were carried out when calculations had to be made using, at best, comparatively simple mechanical aids. Now it is possible to use electronic computers for such work, and the extraction of an increasing number of factors no longer involves a prohibitive amount of time and effort. Using the new aids, Digman (1962) analysed the scores on an opinion survey based on 39 statements similar to those in Eysenck's list. The subjects were 149 residents of Hawaii, and most of them were second-generation Americans of Oriental ancestry, who thus had a different cultural background from the subjects of the other studies mentioned in this chapter.

Eight attitude factors were extracted, which, after consideration of the loadings in these factors of the individual items, were tentatively named as follows:

1. Authoritarian beliefs and attitudes *vs.* Humanitarianism.
2. Equalitarianism.
3. Social liberalism *vs.* Social conservatism.
4. Religionism.

Attitudes: Organisation

5. Political liberalism *vs.* Political conservatism.
6. Nationalism.
7. Tendermindedness *vs.* Toughmindedness.
8. Sex permissiveness.

A point of interest which emerged is that only one of Digman's factors is in agreement with those postulated in earlier studies. This is Factor 7, tendermindedness *vs.* toughmindedness, and so far it is the only one discovered which appears to be culturally invariant. Digman made the suggestion that this may be because it is concerned with aggressiveness, a very widespread human characteristic.

The absence in these two analyses of the factor radicalism-conservatism which has appeared so well-established in studies of Western attitudes is interesting, and points to the conclusion that social attitudes are far more closely related to culture than some authors would lead us to suppose. Keehn (1955) is probably right in asserting that the structure of attitudes in any society may be largely determined by local issues round which attitudes crystallise. When Eysenck (1953a) adduced results from studies of American, Swedish and German subjects as justification for the analysis of social attitudes into two main factors, he was considering results not from different cultural groups but from subgroups of the wider Western culture. Different results appear to accrue when Western and Oriental culture groups are compared.

Digman's study makes it seem likely that the structure of attitudes may be much more complicated than has been assumed in the past. He isolated eight factor dimensions and could have obtained more. In the pre-computer era, analysis on this scale was virtually impossible, and this may have led to the acceptance of very simple factor patterns as adequate. It will be interesting to see what developments in the theory of attitudes follow the use of advanced mechanical aids to computation.

V

ATTITUDE TO AUTHORITY

AMONG THE MANY ATTITUDES which have been studied and analysed in recent years, three stand out as being of more general importance than the rest: the attitude of the individual to authority, his attitude to himself, and the attitude of the members of one group to those of some other group. It is now proposed to study these three attitudes in more detail.

In any society which is not entirely anarchical, there will be some institutions or individuals which are authoritarian in nature. This must be so if the society is to remain in existence, and it is true whether the authority is freely accepted by the members or whether it is superimposed on them against their will. The duty of obedience to something outside oneself has been impressed on nations and individuals from very early times, as is shown by the Old Testament demand for obedience, not sacrifice. In this case the obedience was to God, and authority may be wielded in His name by a priesthood or a Church. This was true in the case of the Jews, who were a theocracy before they were a monarchy, and who have always regarded God as the supreme authority to whom they owe allegiance. In the case of Christendom, there was a like claim, but the Christian Church grew up in secular states, and Christians acknowledged the authority of both Church and state, while considering that each derived its authority from God.

Within the state there are numerous smaller authorities, and it is with these that individuals are likely to be in contact. The most obvious is the family, and in particular the parents, who exercise authority over their children. For children, too, the school is an obvious authoritarian body. Others which might be mentioned are employers, trades unions, and the various societies, religious and secular, which individuals join and whose rules they accept.

The question of what makes some people accept authority easily while others rebel furiously is important. In a school class, there will nearly always be found a majority of children who generally obey the rules but break them on occasion, and there will also be minorities who behave in other ways. A few will just flout rules, and the imposition of a new rule will be the signal for them to break it, even if they have never before thought of the particular misdeed involved. Teachers are painfully aware of these children, and may spend a disproportionate amount of time and effort in attempting to bring them to a different frame of mind. Equally nonconforming, but usually less observed, are the over-docile children who accept unquestioningly all regulations and are never disobedient. They may get less than their due share of attention or they may be held up as shining examples of what pupils should be like. Disapproval is unlikely to come their way, and their teachers are not likely to worry about them enough, often not realising how abnormal their behaviour is.

In adult society different reactions to authority are just as marked as they are among children. Taking radicalism-conservatism and tendermindedness-toughmindedness as basic attitudes, Eysenck (1960) has described four distinct types which he calls toughminded conservative, toughminded radical, tenderminded radical and tenderminded conservative. The first and last of these are those who may be expected to accept authority and favour the *status quo*. In their ranks, but at opposite extremes, Eysenck places both fascists and active churchgoers. The two radical groups he identifies as, on the one hand, communist, and on the other, pacifist.

After the Second World War, some studies were made of the background factors connected with fascist attitudes. The conclusion reached was that potential fascists are the product of a cultural climate acting on individuals of particular types. The conventional type of fascist tended to take over current judgments uncritically and to react to stereotypes. For him, prejudice was a matter of course. The authoritarian type made his social adjustment by accepting obedience and subordination willingly. He held a blind belief in authority and was willing to attack the weak and any others who were acceptable to society as victims. (Adorno, 1960.) Both these types are found among children in schools, and the danger is that they may even be considered good pupils. They learn their lessons and keep the rules without ever asking whether their teachers are right, and they may lull those teachers into a false sense of security. The authoritarian type may be less well-liked because he has a propensity to bully others weaker than himself, and he may also be a toady.

By contrast, the genuine liberal is much more outspoken. He does not accept authority blindly, but is more independent in his thinking, showing moral courage and a desire for personal self-direction. He is likely, too, to be on the side of the underdog. Bass (1963) has suggested that the tendency to acquiesce, which is not equally strong in everyone, may be an important factor in social attitudes and personal behaviour.

The part played by intelligence in the development of conservative attitudes has been investigated by several writers, but their findings are inconclusive. Thurstone (1934), reporting the work of T. G. Thurstone, claimed that the more intelligent students tended to be radical or liberal in their views on social and religious topics. Patriotism was found to be negatively correlated with intelligence. Jones (1938) was much less definite, although still finding a tendency for high intelligence and liberal attitudes to go together. There did not seem, however, any grounds for thinking that it would be possible to predict liberalism from a knowledge of intelligence level, or that liberal views could necessarily be taken as indicative of high intelligence.

The effects of intelligence depend to a great extent on the material on which it has to work, and this is to be found in the environment as well as in the individual himself. Krout and Stagner (1939) found that the more radical students thought of themselves as having been rejected by their parents. There was no objective check on the truth of this state of affairs, the important point being that this was what the radicals believed about their relations with their parents. As seen by them, the home environment had been hostile, and they reacted accordingly, carrying their hostility over as a reaction to society at large.

This could, of course, have been a neurotic reaction, but no evidence was found that the radicals were neurotic. They did seem to be socially maladjusted, though, finding it difficult to meet people and showing a good deal of pessimism. They were more likely to assume their own inferiority than were non-radicals, but also to claim more special abilities. Much later, Eysenck (1951a) supported the finding that radicalism is not linked with emotional instability.

Although not going quite so far as to agree unreservedly with Gilbert and Sullivan on the prenatal origins of liberalism and conservatism, there is fair ground for assuming that the roots of attitudes to authority are to be found in family life. Within the family, authority derives from the parents, and the attitudes of the children both to their parents, and later to the outside society, may depend on the kind of authority the parents exercise and the way they do it. A young child is extremely dependent on its parents, particularly its mother, and the care, or lack of care, which it receives may have a lasting effect on its personality and its adjustment to society in general. It is a tribute to parents that so many young people grow up with feelings of warm affection for them, and that so few actively dislike their parents.

Evidence for this is found in a number of surveys of the opinions of young people below the age of twenty. In one such study, carried out among Youth Clubs in many parts of Britain the writer found that, of the whole group of nearly two thousand questioned, the majority aged between thirteen and twenty, practically all expressed considerable affection for their parents (Evans, 1960). Comments were of the type: 'I honour and trust them, and I am truly thankful for what they have done for me,' and 'I love them for all the things they have done for me, for being always by my side when I was ill, for keeping me the right side of the law, for being the best parents I could ask for.'

Girls throughout the age range considered showed more affection for their parents than did boys, and mothers were regarded with stronger affection than were fathers. Feeling for their fathers, even when no hostility was expressed, tended to lack the positive quality of that for their mothers, and this was recognised, at least tacitly, by the young people themselves. A boy of nineteen wrote: 'I am fond of my parents because my mother is always good to me and my dad generally leaves me alone,' and a sixteen-year-old girl said: 'I love my mother because I can talk freely with her. She helps me and advises me, and is interested in all my activities. My father is constantly finding fault with me.'

Affection for parents was found to drop in intensity between fourteen and twenty, but even so, the large majority remained at least quite fond of one or other of their parents. Only 1·3% of the group expressed dislike for their mothers but when this occurred the feeling was often very strong. One boy, aged seventeen, having taken a job which gave him a home as well as work, explained his reasons thus: 'It's so that I won't have to live with my mother. I have never lived with her and I don't want to. I was at boarding schools until I started work, so she never got to know me. I would not confide in her or bring her my troubles because she has never troubled about me. She was never married.'

Fathers engendered more dislike than mothers, but, even so, very few said they disliked their fathers. Sometimes this was because fathers were thought to be too strict. A girl of sixteen said: 'Dad doesn't know I go out with boys. If he did I would not be allowed to go out.' Her mother, who did know, aided and abetted her in this, and was loved accordingly.

Dislike of parents sometimes arose because they showed

50

little affection for their children and were not interested in them as people. One eighteen-year-old boy illustrated this. 'Being born into a business house, affection was completely forgotten. Dad always had a lot on his mind, and ever since I can remember has never sat down and had a conversation. In fact he has not spoken to me for the last three years except to comment on business. And I have had enough of that by six o'clock.'

These, however, are exceptional cases, and only a small proportion of the young people actively disliked or felt frustrated by their parents. Most recognised and were grateful for the care and encouragement they had received, and appreciated that their parents wanted them to get on in life. 'They want me to make a good position in life, since they themselves have not managed it,' is a typical remark, and so is 'They never forced me to study for exams (even though I did), and they never bribed me. But they never went out and left me alone when I was small.'

Support for these findings comes from an enquiry among school leavers carried out by Birkbeck College students and reported by Veness (1962). Expressions of gratitude to parents were common and expressions of hostility were extremely rare. Parents were seen as a source of strength in trouble, but, although the ties with them were close, there was no sign of excessive dependence. These young people had the secure relationship with their parents which made them look forward to their own future freedom with confidence.

Another survey was carried out among Sixth Form pupils in grammar and public schools in England and Wales, and it is claimed that 16,000 questionnaires were returned and analysed. The interesting point about this survey is that it was conducted and presented by the sixth-formers themselves (*Sixth Form Opinion*, June 1962). The results showed that these young people, all highly intelligent, were of the opinion that their parents had made a good job of bringing them up. Asked to give their parents a mark out of ten, the average for the group was eight. Deep appreciation of the parents' efforts was expressed by many, and only a small minority showed marked disapproval.

Asked whether they thought that, on the whole, their parents treated them as people of their own age should be treated, about three-quarters thought that their fathers did treat them correctly, and slightly fewer of the boys and more of the girls were satisfied with the treatment they got from their mothers. Some of them thought that their parents, especially their mothers, tended to nag them, and some resented being pumped about their activities.

Relations with their parents were formal in the sense that the children, except for a very small minority, did not call the parents by their christian names, but quite a high proportion of the parents did confide in their children. According to the children, 54% of the fathers and 70% of the mothers confided in their sons, and the corresponding figures for daughters were 34% and 78%. The closer relationship with mothers, already noted, is seen again here and is supported by the claim that, if in trouble, 30·7% of the boys and 31·2% of the girls would go to their mothers as against 17·1% and 3·5% who would go to their fathers. The rest would either keep their troubles to themselves or go to someone outside the family for help and advice.

On specific topics, there was some disagreement with parents expressed. Between half and two-thirds of the group shared their parents' views on religion. A little over half agreed with their parents on politics, and a little under half on sex. Aesthetics, as might be expected, showed a greater divergence of opinions between the generations. A little over a third of the fathers and children agreed on this subject, with something over 40% of mothers and children agreeing.

Fifty-seven per cent of both boys and girls thought their parents knew them pretty well, and only a minority thought their parents were underestimating their potential. All in all, the relations between parents and children seemed quite satisfactory, and the fact that nearly two-thirds of the boys and girls thought they would bring up their own children as they themselves had been brought up is an eloquent indication that they did not feel that family life, as they knew it, required a great deal of modification. Stresses and strains there may be, and probably always have been, between members of different generations, but, where these occur in the context of a warmly affectionate home, like the majority of those described in these surveys, there is every possibility that the outcome will be good. Fletcher (1962) was probably right in suggesting that we should view cautiously the more lurid reports of the so-called 'teenage revolt.'

In none of these surveys was a scientifically constructed attitude test used. The instruments were questionnaires and the scoring was by counting the yes and no responses. It is difficult to assess this material statistically, but it is interesting to read and suggestive of trends among young people, which may be checked, or further studied, by other more rigid methods.

There is no lack of work in which attitude scales and other standardised tests have been used in the study of relations between parents and children. Most of these studies bring out differences in children's views of their fathers and mothers. Radke (1946) found that preschool children thought their fathers punished more severely than their mothers, though less frequently, but, in spite of this, it was the mother who had most influence on behaviour. After all, small children spend most of their time with their mothers, receiving from them constant care and training and, when necessary, small punishments, and it is in this context that their attitudes are formed. Even in adult life, most people have very different stereotypes of fathers and mothers.

Stagner and Drought (1935) illustrated the different meanings attached to statements about the two parents. 'We're just good friends,' was a favourable statement when said of the father, but not when said of the mother. 'I feel no affection for him, in fact, he frequently annoys me,' was only slightly unfavourable to the father, but its counterpart was definitely unfavourable to the mother.

Attitude to Authority

Fathers were expected to be stern, strong and silent, as well as reserved and distant, so that their moments of unbending were regarded as occasions of rare good fortune. Mothers, on the other hand, were to be adored. They showed affection to the children, who were below them, and their faults were never to be admitted to anyone.

Work of this kind shows the importance in dealing with children of considering separately the influence of fathers and mothers. We tend to think and speak of home influence as if that were unitary, whereas it is, in fact, made up of many smaller influences. Father and mother, brothers and sisters, and even grandparents and other relations and friends, contribute to an influence which is the resultant of their separate influences, and this resultant depends on the adjustments which a child makes to them individually. The common factor in these adjustments is the child himself. Freudian theory suggests that a child is likely to show antagonism to one parent and fixation on the other, but Stagner and Drought found that, in spite of differences in the attitudes to the two parents, there was still a very small correlation between attitudes to father and mother. This might be partly due to the fact that it was the same child who was reacting to each of the parents.

The majority of children accept their parents as rightful authorities and adopt their standards of behaviour, even if they do not always conform to them. Normal children (Jackson, 1950) admit that children are sometimes naughty, and when this happens they have to be punished. This does not mean that the parents are cruel, and the children usually approve of the type of punishment used, even though it does not always result in better behaviour. Such children have a friendly approach to the world and think of people as good rather than bad. In spite of their acknowledged jealousy of brothers and sisters, these are objects of strong affection and are not rejected.

Neurotic and delinquent children do not have this realistic approach. Neurotics tend to believe that children are bad, not good, and that punishment is likely to be over-severe. They are jealous of brothers and sisters and afraid of their parents.

Strangers they regard as dangerous. Delinquents tend to be less involved than neurotics in the feelings of their families. Where neurotics are centred on their families, delinquents tend to move away from them, with normal children standing between these extremes, neither excessively involved nor prematurely detached.

Antagonism of children to parents is dependent on conditions in the home. Conflict is most likely to occur over discipline practices, responsibilities expected of children, or family rules and regulations. (Bath and Lewis, 1962.) Severe and inconsistent treatment by parents will provoke conflict, and may make children become withdrawn and self-sufficient. Adolescents' opinions on how they should be treated are affected by the treatment they themselves receive, and those from lax, as well as those from strict homes, have been found to be more strict in their own attitudes than those from average homes.

There is a strong tendency for children growing through adolescence to identify themselves with their own parents, and Wright (1962) found that secondary modern school children rated their parents as nearer their ideals than they were themselves. Teachers, on the other hand, were further from the ideal self than the children thought they themselves were.

The impression left by all this work is of warm, human relations between parents and their children, of occasional conflict which, while real, does not usually disrupt family feeling seriously, and of a strong element of admiration and appreciation in the attitudes of children towards their parents. The rarer cases of dislike stand out, perhaps because they are not typical, and the tragedy for individuals which they represent should not be minimised, but home and parents are still, in this generation, a potent force for health and happiness in our society. It is a bad mistake for teachers to think that school influences are all-important in children's lives. If home and school are ever in opposition, home influences are more likely to triumph than school ones. Where home and school work together, their influence is likely to be enormous, and for this reason the closest possible co-operation should be encouraged.

This was achieved naturally when teachers tended to live near their schools and took part in the life of the community together with the parents of their pupils. Now that many travel to work from a distance, more contrivance is necessary to bring parents and teachers together, but the effort is well worth making in the interests of the children whom they are both educating.

For most children, the first authority they meet outside their homes is that of school, and they react to this in individual ways. Glassey (1945) found that the great majority of both parents and children thought education important and considered that more money should be spent on it. This was in spite of the fact that many of them were only moderately interested in school, disliking methods, system and teachers. Stacey (1948), like Glassey, investigated the attitudes of grammar school pupils, but found them less critical. Except in isolated cases, her subjects displayed favourable attitudes to school, and these attitudes remained stable over a period of a year. There did not appear to be any significant relationship between attitudes to school and the intelligence and achievement of the pupils or the socio-economic levels of their homes.

Davies (1959) found that attitudes to school were favourable in a secondary modern school, too, though they became less favourable after the first year. The main reasons for approval here were utilitarian and social, not academic, and most of the grumbles were about lessons that were too long, the lack of variety, the amount of writing required, and boring books. Teachers were sometimes said to be too strict, to talk too much, not to understand the pupils and to show favouritism. These were probably not very general or deeply felt annoyances, for few of the children disliked school, except among the second and third year boys, of whom nearly a quarter expressed dissatisfaction.

These findings are in line with those of the much wider survey reported in the Newsom Report (H.M.S.O., 1963). The head teachers who supplied evidence about the attitudes of pupils in their secondary modern and comprehensive schools agreed that the great majority of their pupils were co-operative, and that the picture sometimes presented of 'the blackboard jungle' is overdrawn and inaccurate. The less able pupils present most problems of discipline, but even among them only 10% of the boys and 7% of the girls were described as especially difficult while 55% of both boys and girls in the lower ability groups were considered to be thoroughly co-operative. The more able boys and girls were generally also more co-operative, and of them only 2% were found to be especially difficult as against 72% of the boys and 75% of the girls who were thoroughly co-operative. A minority expressed their rebellion against school discipline by truancy and the neglect of homework, but far more refused to wear school uniform. The general picture is of acceptance of the authority of the schools, with individual pupils expressing complaints about various aspects of school life. This is what is to be expected in any system which attempts to cater for a large section of the population, with their general welfare in mind. Some will be dissatisfied with the results, and many more will wish for minor alterations in the organisation, but the total effect is unlikely to be large-scale rejection of the efforts made on their behalf.

Another aspect of attitude to authority is concerned with attitudes to religion and religious institutions. One such institution is the Church, and an early scale devised by Thurstone and Chave (1929) was designed to measure attitude to the Church. This scale was presented to students, graduate and undergraduate, at the University of Chicago, to some faculty members, and to the Chicago Forum. Of these groups, the divinity students were the most strongly in favour of the Church and the Chicago Forum was the most antagonistic. No definite trends were found among the student groups, and graduates and undergraduates scored at about the same average level, but the scores of the graduates were more widely scattered.

Women were, on the average more favourable to the Church than men, but the spread of scores was much the same for men and women. Roman Catholics were more favourable and less widely dispersed in attitude than Protestants, while the scores made by Jews were more widely spread and, on the average, less favourable than those of either Christian group.

Attitude seemed to be related to Church attendance, those who claimed to attend Church frequently making more favourable scores than those who did not. Self-ratings of attitude, made by using a graphic rating scale, correlated to an extent of $+0.67$ with scores on the attitude scale, and the authors point out that this is as high a relationship as is usually found between the results of psychological tests and their criteria.

One point which struck the authors was that most of their subjects rated themselves as slightly more favourable than their actual test scores would indicate. Subjects who rated themselves as 'neutral' were frequently found to have checked a number of strongly antagonistic statements on the scale. This seems to be in line with the common observation that many people are unwilling to state categorically that they disbelieve in God. Many will only give lip-service to that belief, but, because they have a sneaking fear that God may exist after all, few will come out as definite unbelievers. This probably accounts for the large number of people who, in any survey, are reported as holding religious beliefs, while few are observed to be practising their religion formally and regularly.

In the Survey of Youth Club members already mentioned (Evans, 1960), about half claimed to believe everything in the Bible and more expressed belief in the Gospels. About three-quarters believed that, after death, they would go to heaven or hell. Their church-going, in spite of these expressions of belief, was irregular and declined with age. At fifteen, nearly half said they went regularly, but at nineteen the figure was one-third. At the same time there was a good deal of casual attendance, probably for weddings, christenings and some of the greater festivals, such as Easter and Christmas. Very few admitted that they never went to Church.

The younger children, fourteen and under, were the ones who were most bored by religion, but more of the older ones said they found it meaningless. Some found it inspiring, and some said they found it difficult to practise, like the boy who said it required full concentration. Anyone who has tried to take Christianity seriously would agree fully with this view.

Girls had a more favourable attitude than boys, and this agrees with the general observation that most congregations contain more women than men. Davies (1959) found the same tendency among his secondary modern school pupils, and thought it sprang from home influences. Boys said their fathers and elder brothers did not go to Church, but girls went with their mothers and elder sisters. Boys tended to dismiss religion as 'kids' stuff' and suspected that grown-ups did not really believe it, though they were not necessarily anti-religious and many liked Sunday School and went to Church clubs. There was a suggestion that this was because these often provided opportunities for summer camping. To girls the singing was an attraction, as it was not to boys once their voices had broken.

Many boys and girls at school understand and appreciate the practical aspects of Christianity. They can accept the idea of Jesus Christ as a good man and find Bible stories interesting, but the more abstract and philosophical aspects of religion elude them, and, because these are intellectually beyond many pupils, they are considered boring or unnecessary. It is only gradually that the hard and fast ideas of right and wrong, good and bad, which children hold give way to more mature concepts, and the pattern of development in this respect is now being studied in work such as that by Goldman (1962).

Some interesting observations on the extent to which people are really certain about their religious beliefs were made by Thouless (1935). He noted a widespread tendency to be more certain than the evidence warranted and a disinclination to regard religious beliefs as more or less probable. This may be because doubt and scepticism are unstable attitudes of mind, and are, for most people, painful. Accordingly, we tend to accept or reject beliefs outright, rather than to take up an intermediate position. Thouless suggested that one aim of a liberal education should be to encourage the development of the ability to take up a more critical position, when this is all the available evidence warrants.

In a much more recent study, Brown (1962) confirmed many of Thouless's findings, and added an analysis of the differences between the members of various religious groups. The common assertion that they differ in personality and attitudes was not supported by the results, where the only significant differences suggested the possibility that students with no religious affiliation might show more anxiety and score lower on authoritarianism than the rest. There was no evidence to support the theory that religious individuals tend to be more neurotic than others.

Factor analysis produced a first factor of religious belief, which was shown to be isolated from opinionative and factual systems and unrelated to personality measures. This factor was positively loaded on institutionalisation and authoritarianism, and negatively on individualism.

The second factor was a personality factor, concerned with anxiety and neuroticism, and positively loaded on opinion strength and factual certainty.

Brown concluded that to maintain a system of religious belief strong social support is required, and adduced as evidence the relationship found between belief and Church membership, attitudes of acceptance of the Church and authoritarianism. Religious beliefs result from social learning, and because beliefs are not susceptible of proof in the same way as factual statements, certainty is possible only when social support for them is forthcoming. Among the young people with whom this study was concerned, Church membership rather than personality was related to strength of belief, and it appeared to be difficult for a highly individualised person to hold conventional beliefs, since he was unlikely to adhere to any institution.

Support for Brown's findings was forthcoming in the work of Hyde (1963). Using a series of carefully constructed tests, measures of attitude to religion and attitude to the Church were obtained from 1977 children (1035 boys and 942 girls) in four schools, boys' and girls' grammar schools and boys' and girls' secondary modern schools, drawing their pupils from approximately the same area of privately owned, semi-detached houses. Six groups were considered, of mean ages from 11.6 to 16.6, and a division was made between those who professed to attend Church at least once a month and those who said they went less than once a month.

When whole age-groups were considered, there was little difference between the mean attitude scores at different ages. Division into church-going and non-church-going groups brought out a pattern. More favourable attitudes to religion were always found among the girls rather than among the boys, but the attitudes of the church-going children whether boys or girls, were always more favourable than those of the rest. Moreover, the church-going children maintained their favourable attitude throughout the age-range studied, while there was a steady decline in the favourableness of the attitude of the non-church-going children. Church-going and a favourable attitude to religion were associated, but no conclusion can be drawn from this as to cause and effect. At the same time, it fits in with Brown's suggestion that a religious attitude needs nurturing in a social milieu.

Another interesting observation made by Hyde is that there was no sudden change in interest in religion during adolescence. The interested were, according to their own estimate, becoming more interested, but there was no evidence for either an age of conversion or sudden conversions. Rather, choices were being made in accordance with a pattern of development.

An obvious criticism of this last piece of work is that it is a cross-sectional study, dealing with a series of age-groups. While it gives useful pointers, it needs to be associated with longitudinal studies of individual children before authoritative statements about lines of development can be made and accepted. Individual trends and differences are all too easily masked when only averages for groups are presented. Patterns of development vary, and individuals mature at very different rates, and to deal with chronological age groups in these times is rather naive. But when that has been said, and the statements about trends in religious attitude discounted, Hyde's evidence of the way in which attitude is maintained among the church-going, and falls away among those separated from the Church is of considerable interest. Jones (1962) reported a similar state of affairs, and included in his study some work on social class and attitudes to church-going. Dividing his subjects, all fourth-year pupils in A streams in mixed grammar schools in South Wales, into four groups according to the occupations of their fathers, he found that in the highest group the attitudes of boys and girls were similar. Moving down the social scale, he found that the attitudes of the girls improved while those of the boys deteriorated.

It is interesting to compare the findings from the studies already mentioned, all carried out in predominantly Christian countries, with some obtained where a different type of religious background prevailed. Vinacke, Eindhoven and Engle (1949) used as subjects students at the University of Hawaii. Hawaii has a very heterogeneous racial composition and the religious groups found there include Mormonism, Buddhism, Shintoism, Confucianism and Taoism as well as Catholic and Protestant Christianity, but Judaism is almost non-existent there.

In this society, the majority of the 577 students questioned professed belief in a deity, many held that Christ is divine and most of the rest that he was a great prophet or teacher. They regarded religion as a natural human function, and said that religion had influenced their upbringing. Most of them reported a gradual religious awakening at about the age of sixteen, rather than sudden conversion, and this agrees with Hyde's finding.

The pattern of shift from one religion to another was studied, and considerable movement was found in Hawaii, particularly from Buddhism into other religions. Buddhism, Shintoism and Confucianism were losing members in this student body, but all other religious groups were gaining. The changes were being made quite peacefully, and without self-consciousness or conflict, but they were quite definite.

Attitude to Authority

As in the other studies, women were found to be more religious than men, and most students reported their mothers as being stronger in faith than their fathers, with themselves standing at an intermediate point.

All this work suggests that the interest of young people in religion is quite real, though their attachment to a Church is less certain. It is interesting to note that those who have been brought up in church-going families and themselves go to church, tend to maintain their favourable attitudes, while attitudes of those who have not had this experience deteriorate as they get older. This is probably an example of the tendency noted earlier, for imposed behaviour to affect attitude development. Children of church-going parents are not only exposed to an atmosphere favourable to church-going, but they also take part in related activities. Accordingly they tend to develop attitudes to religion and the Church which are more favourable than those of children who do not have these experiences. This is another aspect of the importance of family attitudes which supplements what has been said earlier.

VI

ATTITUDE TO THE SELF

A CHILD'S ATTITUDE to other people, both those in authority and his own equals, is likely to depend on his feelings about himself. If he is confident of his own ability to look after himself and cope with the problems of his own life, he will be able to meet other people in a cheerful and friendly way. The child who distrusts himself will be timid and shrinking and is likely to find social contacts difficult and unpleasant. This, in turn, is very likely to have an adverse effect on everything he does, in and out of school, so it is of prime importance that a child should be helped to build up a healthy attitude to himself if his happiness and his efficiency are not to suffer.

Children are born with potentialities for development, but the direction in, and the extent to which, they develop depends on the treatment they receive. Society makes children into the kind of people it wants them to be, placing ideals before them and encouraging them to become like those ideals. Children, more than adults, are constantly being made to compare themselves with ideal people, who often do not exist except in the minds of parents and teachers. Most children know very well the kind of boys and girls of whom their teachers approve, and the teachers themselves might be very surprised at some of these stereotypes. It is good to ask, from time to time, what kind of people we want our pupils to become and to consider whether we are really going the right way about commending our ideas to them.

It is sometimes suggested that we ought not to be training children to conform to any particular pattern, but should leave them free to grow in their own ways. In a civilised community this is impossible. If we did this, we should end up with a lot of little savages who would have no place in our world, and who would be unhappy themselves and a cause of unhappiness to others. Children have a great need to belong, and this is best satisfied by helping them to fit into the society in which they are born. They have to learn to see themselves as individuals in relation to others in their own community.

Awareness of himself as an individual is something a child has to learn. In the beginning, he is physically united to his mother, and it is only at birth that his separate existence begins. As his perceptions of the world around him are organised, he discovers that he and his mother are not one, but two, and that each is distinct from other objects in the environment. His eyes develop their capacity to focus on a moving object, they follow the movements of his hand and, from the sensations he receives when it touches something hard or warm, he recognises it as part of himself. By degrees his sense of his own physical identity is built up. Growing older, he learns that he is a person, and forms a picture of himself based on his own perceived characteristics and on the reactions of other people to him.

In time, the developing child learns he is not only physically separate from other people, but that he also has separate needs, purposes and intentions. In the process of pursuing these, he learns something of his own capacities and, sooner or later, he clashes with other people. From them he receives both encouragement and frustration and he adapts his own behaviour accordingly. The pictures of 'me and mine' and 'you and yours' take shape.

Probably one of the first things a child learns about himself is his name. Most people, asked 'Who are you?', will reply with their names, and the name is seen as a symbol for the person. Children seem to think that a teacher who knows their names knows them, and, for this reason, it is not a waste of teaching time to spend part of the first lesson with a strange class in learning their names. There is no surer way to establish sound relations with pupils than by being able to address them correctly by name, and this is as true of college students as of infant school children.

There is nothing new in the idea that names represent personal qualities. Lists of names and their meanings make popular reading. Recently a piece of work was published which was concerned with the characteristics associated with certain Christian names, and Sheppard (1963) found that the tendency to associate characteristics with names was quite real. John was trustworthy, Robin was young, Tony was sociable, Agnes and Matilda were not good-looking, Agnes was not young. Of the names listed, John and Ann suggested the most desirable characteristics.

In this work, none of the subjects commented on his or her own name. It might be interesting to try to find out whether agreement exists between holders of the same name about the characteristics they associate with it.

Long before he starts school, a child has a picture of himself and knows who he is. This self-image is a complex, made up of the child's picture of his bodily self, his personality and character qualities, and his perception of his own status. 'I am John.' He also has an appreciation of the way in which others see him. 'Mummy says I am a good boy.' 'Daddy says I'm smart.' 'David says I'm greedy – or too small – or a little pest.' It is true that the child may not be right in his view of what others think of him, but it is his view of this that affects his development and behaviour.

At some stage a child begins to have ideals. He wants to please his parents or someone else, to be the kind of person they admire. 'Mummy likes good boys.' Sooner or later, he develops ideas about the kind of person he himself would like to be. 'I want to be clever like Daddy,' becomes 'I want to be clever.' He may set out to become the kind of person he wants to be. The ideal self has been born.

During adolescence a change in the self-concept has to take place if maturity is to be achieved. From seeing himself as a child, the individual has to learn to see himself as an adult.

Attitude to the Self

A dependent self has to become independent, and the success with which this is done is partly the result of the treatment which the boy or girl receives from others. If parents and teachers acknowledge a developing competence to deal with problems, to make decisions and to take responsibility, the transition from child to adult is likely to be comparatively smooth. It is probably made more easily by young wage-earners than by their contemporaries who are still at school, for financial independence is demonstrable as intellectual independence may not be.

The importance attached to the idea of the self is obvious from the amount of theorising which has taken place about it. Philosophers, psychologists, sociologists and educationists have all written at length on the subject.

In Mead's (1934) opinion, a child has no 'self' at birth, and its development is dependent on social experience and activity. Mead sees the self as a structure of attitudes, built up, partly, by the organisation of the perceived attitudes of others towards himself and towards one another in social acts and situations, and, partly, by the organisation of the generalised attitudes of the social group to which he belongs. It is only as a member of a community that an individual can be a self, and he possesses a self only in relation to the selves of other members of the group to which he belongs. A child living from birth in complete isolation, if that were possible, would never develop a self, because there would be no others with whom he could interact socially. Man is not innately self-conscious, and he only learns to regard himself as an object because he is one to other people with whom he has social communication.

Because we belong to many groups, we develop many selves. The attitudes of other members of the family towards a child may be separate and different from the attitudes he encounters at school, and it is common observance that a child may present a very different picture at school from that which his parents see at home. When he gets older, social and work groups may call into being yet other selves.

Mead's theory can be seen in relation to that of Freud (1933 and 1949). In Freud's scheme, the original system of personality is the *id*, made up of all the psychological material which is inherited and present at birth. This is an inner world of experience, subjective and separate from reality, which seeks relief from excitation and tension in accordance with the pleasure principle. Because the individual lives in a real world, the *ego* comes into existence as a means of communication between the id and objective reality. It is said to operate in accordance with the reality principle, which suspends the pleasure principle and, by means of thinking, the ego tests reality and controls action in the interests of the preservation both of the individual and the species.

In addition to the id and the ego, Freud postulated the *superego*, representing internally the values and ideals of the society to which the child belongs. Originally, these are conveyed through its parents by means of rewards and punishments meted out in response to its behaviour, but they later become incorporated into its ego-ideal by the process of introjection. In this way self-control is established and the individual becomes self-critical. The superego works in opposition to the id, in that it inhibits natural impulses, and to the ego, in that it substitutes moral goals for realistic ones.

To Adler, the important factor in the development of the self was the style of life, and he offered this as an explanation of the differences between individuals. Everyone, according to Adler (1930), wishes to be superior, but we do not all attempt to be so in the same way. We do not all have the same style of life. This is formed by the setting, in early childhood, of attitudes and feelings which can be changed later only with great difficulty, and which help to make us unique as persons. At one stage, Alder considered that the style of life was the result of attempts to compensate for specific inferiorities, but he later inclined more to the view that the overriding impulse came from what he called the creative self. Man, according to this theory, is self-determining, making his own personality out of the raw material of his heredity and experience, and the creative self ensures that the result is dynamic and unique. There is here a conception of man as striving consciously for personal goals which is absent from the theory of Freud.

It is important that the goals for which an individual strives should be realistic. Whether they are or not will depend on the idealised image of himself which he creates, and Horney (1946) has stressed the danger of an unrealistic image. The more unrealistic the image, she said, the more vulnerable does the individual become and the more avid for outside affirmation and recognition. This is typical of neurotics. We do not need to have qualities of which we are certain confirmed in this way. In an extreme case, the individual may convince himself of his own superiority or, alternatively, a realisation of the differences between himself and the idealised image may lead to extreme self-disparagement. In contrast to genuine ideals, such an image has no dynamic quality and is a hindrance to growth because it prevents an acknowledgment of real shortcomings or inhibits attempts at overcoming them.

In contrast to theories such as these, much recent experimental work seems to go back to the views on the constituents of the self propounded by William James in his *Principles of Psychology* in 1890. James considered these constituents to be (1) the material self, consisting of the individual's material possessions including his body, (2) the social self, or the recognition received from others, (3) the spiritual self, the inner or subjective being, and (4) pure Ego, the stream of thought which makes up the individual's sense of personal identity. A great deal of educational research has investigated the child's beliefs about himself, what he believes other people think about him, and his ideal self or himself as he would like to be.

The methods used for studying attitudes to the self are varied. With children at school, essays on suitably chosen topics may provide useful information without arousing the pupils' suspicions of their purpose. Questionnaires provide a more direct approach and are consequently more open to deliberate faking, but they have the advantage of obtaining, more or less unequivocally, the information required, without also obtaining less relevant material from which it must be separated. Either essays or questionnaire responses tend to result in the picture of the self which the writer wishes to display, but they should not be entirely ruled out because of this, for the picture the subject wishes to present is a construct worthy of very serious consideration.

Less direct approaches can be made through projection tests, and by their use the skilled investigator may obtain considerable insight into the values of the subject about himself, both as an individual and in relation to his social and physical world. This work is largely clinical, and may be based on standard tests such as the Rorschach and TAT, or on projective material developed for a particular piece of research. A clinical method from which a theory of the self has been developed is Rogers's client-centred therapy, which aims at changing the subject's view of himself by accepting him as he is unconditionally, so that he becomes aware of his own feeling and attitudes and so is enabled to live his experience of the moment more completely and to become a fully functioning person. (Rogers, 1959 and 1961.)

One of the methods used by Rogers and his associates for studying the self is Stephenson's Q-technique. (Stephenson, 1936a, b, c.) A packet of statements has to be sorted in various ways so as to show the characteristics of the subject. In addition to sorting to show what he thinks of himself at the moment, they may also be sorted to show what he thinks he was like or will be like at a particular age, what he wishes he were like, and how he thinks he appears to others. Treatment of the results by inverted factor analysis follows, and comparisons between the various pictures of the self produced in this way may be useful and illuminating.

Several studies of children's attitudes to themselves follow a pattern laid down by Jersild (1952). Material obtained from essays written by children on 'What I Like About Myself' and 'What I Dislike About Myself' was analysed so as to yield information about their attitudes to such aspects of the self as physical characteristics, clothing and grooming, health, home and family, ability in sports, school, intellectual abilities, special talents, personality, social attitudes and relationships, and religion.

An expectation that some categories might be used more at some age levels than at others was not fulfilled. If a category of self-description was widely used at one age, it was likely to be widely used at others also, although the details might change with age. This was particularly true where feelings and attitudes were involved, and this is not really surprising when one thinks of the intensity of grief or disappointment, joy or mirth, fear or anger shown by quite small children. The occasions producing displays of these feelings may change in character with age, and so may their modes of expression, but the feelings themselves exist, and are recognised for what they are, very early in life. Emotional experience cuts across age groups and differences of intelligence, sex, education and status, so that grief and exaltation may be felt by a whole nation, and a whole school may thrill with pride. Thus the teacher who understands himself and his own feelings can also understand the feelings of his pupils. We are indeed members one of another.

When the children's responses were analysed, the greatest number were found to be concerned with personality, character, temperament, emotional moods and tendencies. Self-evaluations were often, but not always, subjective, for they included cases where assessment was in terms of an outside standard or code. Some liked themselves because their morals were good, others thought their morals were good because they liked themselves.

Another large category of responses was concerned with social relationships and attitudes towards others. Here there was a tendency, stronger among the older than the younger subjects, to see themselves as they thought others saw them. The suggestion was made that the attitudes a person has towards others are likely to reflect his attitude to himself.

Intellectual abilities were not as prominent as might have

been expected, and in their self-evaluation these children mentioned other qualities more frequently. It was thought that this might be because the normal person sees himself more on an emotional than on an intellectual basis, and comes to terms with himself through feeling rather than thinking. The college students stressed intellectual ability more than the rest, and were inclined to think well of their intellectual abilities. In the education of normal children, it may be that we are likely to find a common basis on the emotional and social level rather than the intellectual.

Special talents seemed to be more important than intellectual abilities. They liked their ability to paint or sing, or play an instrument, to play a game or act. These seem to be the activities which make children see themselves as individuals, mark them out from the rest, more surely than general intellectual ability. A good teacher will always make use of the special talents of his pupils wherever possible, and this is sound practice.

Physical characteristics were also freely mentioned as being liked or disliked by their possessors. Early adolescence was the age at which this was most true. Among older subjects the emphasis was more often on total impression or general appearance, while younger ones were more likely to describe particular features. Actual size was mentioned more often among dislikes than likes. Shortness mattered to boys and fatness to girls. Possibly younger children, had they been included, would have expressed more views about their physique, which is often commented on during early years. A child often hears himself described as big or small for his age, but this is less common once adult size is reached. Provided there is no great abnormality, most adults appear to accept their size and only the very small man or very large woman shows obvious signs of dissatisfaction or embarrassment, and even this is not always so.

Jersild's enquiry was carried out in the United States, and it was soon followed by others there, such as that described by Strang (1957). Similar enquiries were carried out in Britain by Forrester (1951), Staines (1958), Emmett (1959), Mistry (1960) and Lahiry (1960).

It is plain that children are aware of their own development and have a conscious desire to develop in particular ways. They do not all want to develop in the same direction, but this universal desire for development means that there is always something to which they will respond if the growing point can be found and used. The picture which boys and girls have of themselves is formed at quite an early age and increases in stability as they get older.

It is unusual for a child to have an entirely negative picture of itself, though children are often self-critical and dissatisfied with themselves in some ways. Where a child is over-critical of himself, there is often an adverse family background to be taken into account.

School failure is another factor which can make children uncertain of themselves, and so can anxiety over school work. Children following a course of their own choice and enjoying it are likely to develop a healthy self-picture, and under these conditions the apathy so often seen in pupils nearing the end of a secondary school course may be avoided.

The attitudes of their teachers can also influence pupils' self-pictures. A teacher who encourages children by an appreciation of their skills can help them to a clear assessment of their strengths and weaknesses, and so to a knowledge of their own adequacy. The actual competence of the teacher is not the factor which decides the effect, but the method of approach to the children as people. The teacher who values his or her pupils and treats them with respect makes a real contribution to their personal adjustment. Whether or not the teacher is aware of what is happening, the methods of teaching used and the relationships between teacher and pupils help to determine the children's pictures of themselves.

Knowledge of one's own abilities is likely to be at least as important as knowledge of one's own personality characteristics. Arsenian (1942) found that students who made gross mistakes in their estimates of themselves were likely to provide a disproportionately great number of problem cases during their college careers, and Torrance (1954) obtained similar results. Students entering college usually tended to over-estimate their abilities considerably, and it is easy to understand that this tendency may lead to disappointment and distress later. It is possible to help people to improve their self-knowledge, and Johnson (1953) found that this could be done more successfully in respect of objective qualities, like intelligence and interests, than of personality qualities. Pupils should always be encouraged to go as far as they can in their studies, but it is not kindness to allow them to develop an inflated idea of their own capabilities, and the end result of this may be tragic disillusionment later.

As has already been noted, most people are aware of a number of different 'selves', and it is interesting to enquire whether the individual's view of himself corresponds with the way in which he believes others see him, and whether either of these approximates to the ideal self that he would like to be. Brownfain (1952) found that, among men students, stable self-concepts were associated with good adjustment, fewer inferiority feelings and less nervousness, and greater popularity. Students with stable self-concepts saw themselves more as they thought others saw them, were more active socially and showed less compensatory defensive behaviour.

If one assumes that boys and girls try to become like their ideals, then these are likely to have considerable effect on their development. In a society where the roles of men and women are fairly sharply differentiated, it is not to be expected that boys and girls will have quite the same ego-ideals, but they do, to a great extent, admire the same qualities. Wright (1962) found that the main difference, where children of about fourteen were concerned, lay in the tendency of boys to value achievement highly while girls stressed more the qualities of personal relationships. Both valued happiness, but while boys emphasised the importance of skill, adventurousness and cleverness, girls stressed popularity, patience and trustfulness. Boys did not want to be calm, hard, peaceful or ordinary, and girls did not want to be ordinary, knowledgeable, calm or soft, while both sexes ranked wealth low in importance. It is easy to see here the influence of the male and female stereotypes approved in our society.

Somewhat older boys and girls see themselves in relation to their future marriage partners, and Evans (1960) has reported the opinions of some youth club members. Almost all thought that to love and be loved was the most important thing in marriage, but they were quite aware that personal qualities had to be taken into consideration too. Asked what they thought they themselves should be like in order to make their marriage partners happy, they mentioned respect, love of children, being a good cook, understanding, faith and trust, help in difficulties, being of the same religion, not being given to nagging, trustfulness and kindness as desirable. From their partners they wanted tolerance, good manners, skill in love-making, the ability to succeed and willingness to help in the home. A high salary came low in the list of qualifications, but good taste, a sense of humour and coming from the same social level were mentioned by some.

It appeared that the girls saw the ideal wife as a person who loves her husband, is able to see a joke, is well dressed and well mannered, and tolerant. The boys considered a good husband should love and help his wife, be a good lover, be successful enough to earn a good salary, and be generous with his money. Each should have the important qualities of the other, but in a lesser degree. These are evidently the ideals towards which boys and girls wish to grow as they approach adulthood.

So far, two kinds of self-knowledge have been considered in this chapter. Firstly, there is the individual's knowledge of himself and his own powers. 'I can read – or count – or knit – or ride a bicycle.' 'I am patient – or clever – or quick-tempered.' Then, secondly, there is his estimate of himself in relation to others. 'I can run faster than John. I am not as clever as Tony.' Both types of self-knowledge are important.

Unless a child knows what he can and cannot do, he may

spend his time attempting what is, for him, impossible, while at the same time neglecting other tasks at which he could be successful. Instead of enjoying and increasing his own proficiency, he may be constantly frustrated by failure which is, in no sense, his own fault. On the other hand, a clever child may set his sights too low, and spend his time working well below the level of his own capacity. Children of both these types are to be found in most schools, and it should be one of the tasks of their teachers to help them form better estimates of their own capacities.

But we are not only individuals, we are also members of groups, large and small, and it is necessary and inevitable that we should compare ourselves with other people. The system of division of labour gives opportunities for the use of a great diversity of talents, and the common good depends on as many people as possible doing the tasks for which they are best fitted. Some will be fitted to hold high office, others will be needed to perform more lowly tasks. The main object of guidance, either educational or vocational, is to try to fit round pegs into round holes, in the belief that there they will be both useful and happy.

One of the marks of maturity is an acceptance of oneself as one is. Before this state of affairs can exist, it is necessary to have a true picture of oneself, and this should develop bit by bit. Schools can help children to get to know their own powers and to see themselves in relation to their own contemporaries, and the way in which they do this is important. Sometimes we all have to learn through failure, but no child should have to learn continually in this way. Knowledge of what he can do should compensate for the things he cannot do, and the shattering of a child's confidence in himself as a person is to be avoided at all costs. The most important factor in the education of any child is his acceptance by those around him, as he is, with deficiencies as well as capabilities, better than some, less good than others, but always as himself, someone who has a place in his own community which no one else can fill.

VII

INTERGROUP ATTITUDES

AFTER A CHILD has learnt to see himself as an individual and in relation to his parents, he becomes aware of the other people around him. Very early in life, he learns that he is a member of his own family, and that the family is a unit to which some people belong while others do not. In short, the child acquires his first ideas of the ingroup and the outgroup, of 'we' and 'they'. Feeling and behaviour towards ingroup members differ from those towards outsiders, and links with the former are not easily to be broken and are often considered to be permanent, not to be broken, or even not breakable, in any circumstances. Certainly genetic relationships between parents and children or between siblings cannot be changed, even though social relationships may be.

As a child grows older, he participates in the life of other groups as well as of the family and develops prejudices, some favourable, some not, towards people who do not belong to the same groups as himself. Very often groups are formed because their members have common purposes or common interests, and it is not at all unusual to find their members holding common opinions on many topics. In a political club, for instance, the members are likely to hold opinions about government which are sufficiently similar to ensure that they all vote for the same party in a parliamentary election. On other subjects they might differ quite considerably. In this case, the members of the club have come together because of their common opinion about politics. In a sports club, it is interest in a particular game or sport which brings the members together. They all agree that this is a delightful activity, but they are unlikely to agree about politics. The members of any group are likely to hold fairly homogeneous opinions about the activity which brought them together, but on other topics their opinions are likely to be much more heterogeneous. Nevertheless, groups do tend to see themselves as units and to feel that they differ in important ways from other groups. There can be very strong prejudices between groups, and sometimes this issues in hostile behaviour. Examples range from the gang warfare of children's groups to war between nations.

Two different types of prejudice between groups must be distinguished. The first of these is the feeling which exists between groups which are, and remain, distinct. These may be national groups, such as Americans and Russians, or groups within a large community, such as English Protestants and English Roman Catholics, the pupils of two secondary schools in the same town, or the members of different families in the same village. The second is the feeling of the members of a group towards outsiders who are introduced into the group. Immigrants or refugees entering a country and remaining in it would exemplify this. So would new children entering an existing class or school, whether they were or were not of the same race as the original pupils. In this case, there is the problem of assimilation to be considered. In the former, only the question of friendly or hostile feelings occurs, since the groups will continue to exist separately, though individual members of them may meet from time to time.

Intergroup feeling is obvious in classroom groups. Once the infant school stage is passed, boys and girls tend to separate and they rarely mix voluntarily again until well into adolescence. Often there is a good deal of rivalry between sex groups, and some adults are unwise enough to foster it. Moreno (1953) gave sociograms showing this type of cleavage. It probably occurs partly because boys and girls are expected to have different interests and they adopt the roles prepared for them by society. Age is another factor influencing group formation. Faunce and Beegle (1948) found that in a farm youth camp there was strong rejection of one another by both the youngest and the oldest groups, and that the middle group rejected the youngest but wished to approach the oldest, whose members, nevertheless, rejected them.

Cleavage between social classes often occurs among adults, but it is less common among children. Sower (1948) and Becker and Loomis (1948) both found parental occupation had little influence on children's friendships and that personal qualities, values and moral standards mattered more. Where children do choose friends of their own social class rather than of other classes, it is frequently because they have more opportunities of meeting them out of school and so developing shared interests and activities. Where opportunities for free mixing are given, children do not generally show much class consciousness unless differences are accompanied by unacceptable personal characteristics.

The feeling between majority and minority groups in the same population may depend on their relative proportions. Where a few minority members join a large group, they are likely to be well received and easily assimilated, but, if the minority is relatively large, it may be rejected. Criswell (1942) has suggested that, besides the size of the minority, the rate at which its members are added to the existing group may affect their reception. If each addition can be assimilated before the next is made, far more may eventually be assimilated than would have been the case if they had all been introduced at the same time. Cleavage is not always due to the action of the majority. Sometimes it occurs because the minority members draw together and form a sub-group instead of mixing freely. This is less possible where there are comparatively few of them, and may be why small minorities or a series of small minorities, are more likely to be assimilated. Teachers know how readily a few new children are usually accepted by a class, and how difficult it sometimes is to weld the more or less equal remnants of two classes into a working unit.

An extremely important intergroup attitude at the present

time is connected with race relations. National and ethnic groups are still observably distinct and possibilities for intergroup aggression are probably greater now than they have ever been in the history of the world. No one who lived as an adult in Western Europe during the period 1930-50 is likely to underestimate the dire results of active anti-Semitism, and today we are being made aware, in no uncertain fashion, of the strength of feeling which exists between peoples of different colours and different ideologies. According to Adorno (1950), ethnocentrism depends on a rigid distinction between the ingroup and the outgroup, between 'we' and 'they'. It involves stereotyped imagery, negative for the outgroup and positive for the ingroup, and the belief in the superiority of one's own group and the inferiority of others. Educationists have not been slow to appreciate the importance of racial attitudes, and studies both of their origin and of the ways in which they can be modified have been made over a number of years.

Nationality preferences have been studied, in the main, by one of two methods. Thurstone (1928) applied his newly developed method of paired comparisons (Thurstone, 1927 and 1959) to an experimental study of racial attitudes. Undergraduates of the University of Chicago were presented with a list of all the possible pairs formed from a list of 21 nationalities, 210 pairs in all, and asked to underline the one of each pair with which they would prefer to associate, and as a result a scale of nationality preferences was produced. Because of the amount of work involved, this method is not easy to use.

The most widely used method of studying preferences is that due to Bogardus (1947), who asked his subjects to express their feelings about members of other race groups by indicating whether they would admit them to close kinship by marriage, to a social club as personal friends, to a street as neighbours, to employment in the same occupation, to the country as fellow-citizens or only as visitors, or whether they would completely exclude them from the country. This method of assessing social distance has since been widely used. In

Bogardus's original study, great differences were found between the warmth of the welcomes likely to be extended to different groups. Bogardus expressed the opinion that racial goodwill was engendered by race connections which were felt to enhance an individual's status, but that prejudice was aroused, and tended to persist, where racial contacts might endanger status or the status of anything valued.

At one time or another, a great many bodies have been set up whose avowed aim has been the improvement of international relations by educational methods. Not surprisingly, a great increase in this type of work occurred between the two World Wars, and a good account of the activities undertaken during the years 1919–39 has been given by Bull (1954). A great deal of energy was devoted to schemes for providing teachers with material on which they could base lessons on internationalism, courses and conferences were arranged, and school celebrations organised, but there does not appear to have been any attempt made at assessing the outcomes. Though the ideas evolved were admirable, we have no means of telling how successful they were in practice.

Other studies, in themselves more humble, have provided more definite and tangible information. In a number of these studies, the subjects have been children, and the aim has been to discover how they think of other peoples and the sources of their prejudices about them. Without exception, their authors have reported the existence of national stereotypes among children, so that many of them will describe the Japanese as cruel, Negroes as lazy and Jews as money-minded, in spite of the fact that they have little or no personal experience of members of these groups.

Green (1932) found that a representative sample of Welsh children, aged from seven to seventeen, spoke with confidence of Chinese, Negroes, the French, Germans, Italians, Spaniards and Americans. Books were the main source of their information, with school, home, newspapers, the cinema, religious sources and personal experience accounting for the rest. Asked to apply descriptive epithets to various national groups, some of the older children occasionally objected that it was not possible to label a whole nation in this way, but all were willing to make some indictments, and the only difference between the seven and the sixteen-year-olds appeared to be that the latter were more ingenious in justifying their prejudices.

It seemed that, by the age of seven, the children were already biased, that this remained true through their whole school career, and that it might be expected to be true through their later lives. The enquiry did not, in fact, provide any information about the beginnings of prejudice, though it amply confirmed its existence.

Examination of the statements made by children showed the recurrence of certain types of answer. Peoples were described as 'good' or 'bad' according as they provided for our pleasure or not. The suggestion was made that this resemblance to a child's experience of his parents is important. The parents are the first people who provide for a child's well-being and are also the first people to punish him, accordingly he feels both love and hate for them. By the age of seven, the same feelings for racial and national groups are apparent. It was suggested that the explanation lies in the way in which foreigners are represented in the social culture of the child's group. While the child learns in time that his parents are human beings, not good or evil giants, he does not so easily experience foreigners as ordinary people. They are too often represented to him by obsolete and fantastic national costumes, by isolated and picturesque historical episodes, or by striking but not typical individuals.

Green's study was carried out in 1932, between the two World Wars, and the children questioned would not have been old enough to remember the 1914-18 War, though some of them would have been born before it ended. It is interesting to compare it with a study reported a few years after the end of the Second World War by James and Tenen (1950). The children who were the subjects of this study did remember the war, and many of them had had first hand acquaintance with prisoners of war in camps near their homes. Their acquaintance with foreigners in general was probably much wider than that of the children in Green's study.

The children in the study by James and Tenen were girls, pupils of one secondary modern school, and they were interviewed and encouraged to talk freely about foreign people. As a result of what they said, assessments were made of their attitudes to members of several national groups.

At the time of this enquiry, the war was still fairly fresh in the memory of the children and obviously affected their opinions of Germans, Italians and Japanese, who had recently been enemies of Britain. They had, however, met German and Italian prisoners of war, and had sometimes had friendly relations with these either in the neighbourhood or as visitors in their own homes. This personal contact had in many cases altered their original attitudes of distrust, and they had realised that Germans and Italians are often likeable and are certainly not always bad. On the other hand, the Japanese, whom they had not met, were still regarded with hostility.

When the opinions expressed by girls who had had personal contact with members of the various groups were compared with those of girls who had only observed them, a significant difference was found in the case of Negroes, Italians and Germans, with smaller differences in the cases of Indians and Americans. In this investigation, personal contact was found to have resulted in the development of more favourable attitudes, but the authors made it quite clear that this need not be invariably true. The quality of the contact is important, and where this is unsatisfactory it may conduce to the formation of less favourable attitudes.

Dislike appeared to be aroused by disturbing items, such as cruelty, torture, ill-treatment of children or prisoners of war, violence, roughness, and, in some cases appearance, colour and speech. Some girls, however, found strange dress and speech attractive rather than alarming.

Items making for liking were of two types, those which were reassuring in that they showed foreigners as not frightening, and those which showed them as socially pleasant, friendly, kind, generous, good-tempered.

It was very noticeable that personal contact would change attitudes based on second-hand experience, though sometimes a conflict was involved. In the majority of cases, peoples were thought of in the same way as individuals, and the girls generalised from their experiences with individuals in forming their opinions of the characteristics of peoples.

Racial conditions in Britain differ considerably from those in the United States, where immigration has produced a large population from many ethnic groups, so that children have contact with United States citizens who have recognisably foreign backgrounds. The attitudes to foreigners of American children of different racial backgrounds were found by Zeligs (1948) to be very similar and the conclusion was drawn that they were moulded by the social environment. Horowitz (1947) and Radke, Sutherland and Rosenberg (1950) came to the same conclusion about attitudes to Negroes. It was the influence of the outside community, they thought, which caused children to acquire, at a very early age, prejudices about Negroes, and only one group of children seemed to be immune. These were the children of communists.

It is obvious that any attempt to reduce racial prejudice in children will have to take account of the attitudes prevailing in the society in which they live. At the same time, it is also obvious that some people appear to be more liable to be prejudiced in particular directions than are others. Much attention has been given to the study of personality characteristics associated with prejudice, and some important accounts of this work are available. Especially noteworthy as a detailed account of a large-scale investigation is *The Authoritarian Personality* by Adorno, Frenkel-Brunswik, Levinson and Sanford (1950), which is concerned mainly with anti-Semitism, but also includes work on ethnocentrism and fascism. This deals with prejudice in adults, but work on prejudice in children has also been reported by Frenkel-Brunswik (1948).

Data were gathered from a large number of children between

the ages of eleven and sixteen and stereotypes of ethnocentric and tolerant children were prepared. From these, it became obvious that parental behaviour played an extremely important part in shaping the children's attitudes. In the case of the ethnocentric children, the parents were greatly concerned with status and used harsh and rigid discipline. The children submitted without acceptance or understanding, and saw the parents as providers for physical needs and capricious arbiters of punishment. Although the children appeared on the surface to idealise their parents, there were underlying feelings of injustice and victimisation and a lack of genuine affection. The children's abilities for love and creative activities were restricted, and they did not acquire an internalised conscience. They became aggressive or delinquent, failed to integrate or express their hostile tendencies, and as a result, developed a narrow and rigid personality.

The tolerant children, on the other hand, having received affection were able to give it, and were less concerned with power and more with love. They had a loving dependence on their parents, and their anxieties, insecurities and conflicts were more open and more directly faced. They feared punishment and retaliation less, and so could accept the values imposed by society. They judged people by their intrinsic worth rather than by their conformity to a social pattern, and could withstand propaganda for the defamation of minorities. Because of their basic security, they did not, like the ethnocentric children, have to project on to the outgroup their specific problems of aggression, underlying weakness or preoccupation with sex. Instead they could evaluate them realistically.

The most important problem in this context was seen to be the child's attitude to authority. Forced submission was likely to result in surface conformity and violent underlying destructiveness, so that frightened children tried to gain security by over-simplifying relationships with others on the basis of crude external characteristics. The conclusion was reached that, in order to bring about the attitude needed for a genuine identification with society, and so for international understanding, an individualised approach to the children, with the right proportions of permissiveness and guidance, and deliberately planned democratic participation in school and family life, was required.

Family life is not under the control of the school and the attitudes generally prevailing in society cannot be changed overnight, so these must be accepted as part of the framework within which children have to be educated. At the same time, one function of education is to produce desirable changes in the general outlook of the population. This is done, in part, by modifying the attitudes of successive generations of children by educational experiences.

Where attitudes to foreigners are concerned, there has been a general assumption that greater knowledge leads to greater tolerance, and many schemes of instruction designed to reduce racial intolerance have been based on this hypothesis. As early as 1932, Peterson and Thurstone used films to try to influence social and international attitudes and obtained encouraging results. More recently, a number of teaching methods designed to produce a sympathetic approach to specific groups of foreigners have been tried out in this country.

James and Tenen (1950), Khan (1954) and Wakatama (1957) all studied the influence on children's attitudes of contact, for brief periods, with foreign teachers. Particular methods of teaching geography were used by Wakatama, and by Feakes (1953). The natural curiosity of children was exploited, and their interest in the lives of children of other nationalities. They were led to see foreigners as people with feelings and needs not so very different from their own, but expressed in different ways because of the conditions in which they live. Care was taken to see that the information given was presented at the level of situations with which the children were familiar in their own lives, so that it took on for them the quality of reality and did not remain remote.

All these studies support the view that attitudes towards foreign peoples can be changed by giving information about them. It is noticeable that, in all cases, care was taken to give favourable information. The foreign teachers sent into the schools were warm, friendly personalities, capable of making good contacts with the children and likely to be acceptable to them. The lessons taught stressed the good qualities of the peoples they dealt with. Of course information of this kind will make a favourable impression. Of course it will result in more favourable attitudes. But what would happen if the children came into contact with a fair cross-section of the population of a foreign country? What would be the result of their acquiring less carefully selected information? Would living with people who were not definitely out to make a good impression, but were carrying on with their own affairs, have any significant effect on attitudes?

Some indication of the answers to these questions may perhaps be gleaned from the work of Jayatilaka (1951). Much less carefully designed than the studies already mentioned, it came nearer to real life than any of them. Here the effect on students of many nationalities, studying at the University of London Institute of Education during the session 1949-50, of living and working together was considered. A test of attitude to internationalism was constructed and applied at the beginning and again at the end of the session. No particular influence was brought to bear on the students, but many of them lived in hostels and there, as in their classes, they met students of nationalities other than their own.

It is cheering to find that this kind of contact appeared to the students themselves to have made them more international-istic in their outlook. They thought that some of their pre-judices had been removed, that they had come to question some of their own values, and had acquired a more sympathetic understanding of different ways of life. They also became more aware of the possibility of tension, and some were confused and perplexed and unable to see how world situations could be eased by improved personal relationships.

In assessing the value of work of this kind, the permanence of any attitude changes noted must be considered. James and

Tenen (1935) found that an improvement in attitude to Negroes resulting from contact with two African teachers was maintained for at least six weeks after their visit to the school. Khan (1954) found that the new attitude remained stable, in some cases, for six months. Miller and Biggs (1958), using a discussion technique with Australian schoolboys, found that a resulting improvement in racial attitudes was held over at least a two-week period. The evidence is slender, but it indicates that the results are not entirely ephemeral.

A curious omission in studies of racial attitudes is that none of the authors appears to have taken into account the children's attitudes to their own countries and nationalities. It is necessary to have some conception of one's own fellow-countrymen before one can have any real feeling about nationals of other countries. What ideas does a child have about its own country? Piaget (1928) noted three stages in the evolution of the idea of country. During the first, a country was seen as a unit, in the same way as a town or village or a district was, and all these were of equal importance and existing side by side. Then towns, villages and districts were considered to be in the country but not parts of it. In the last stage, the correct relationship was understood. Piaget also found that children's ideas of what the word 'foreigner' meant were often vague and inaccurate. At the same time, many of the children could verbalise correctly about their own country and about foreigners, and this often masked their real ignorance of the significance of the terms.

Piaget's work was carried out with Swiss children, but recently Jahoda (1963) made a similar enquiry in Glasgow. Children of Scottish parentage, aged from six to eleven, were found to show a progression from having no conception of Glasgow as a unitary whole, through stages where it was not seen as part of Scotland and Scotland was not seen as part of Britain, to one where the Glasgow-Scotland-Britain relationship could be correctly expressed. The danger that this might be only a verbal exercise was recognised, and an ingenious non-verbal, as well as a verbal, approach was used.

The evidence obtained in this study was of a steady development of understanding, between the ages of five and eleven, of the idea of nationality. The middle-class children appeared to be in advance of the working-class children, but this difference disappeared when they were matched for intelligence, and, as is usual in learning situations, it was concluded that individual and group differences really depended on intelligence differences. Children's ideas about country and nationality depend on their intellectual maturity, and it is unrealistic to neglect this, either in the teaching of geography and history or in investigating their attitudes to other peoples. A child who has not yet achieved a clear idea of his own nationality is unlikely to have any real opinions about other countries, and this may well have been the case with some of the children, in both junior and secondary schools, who were questioned in some of the studies already mentioned. Understanding should not be too readily inferred from apparently intelligent verbalisation.

Language is commonly associated with nationality, and Jahoda found that some of the confusion among his subjects over the idea of Scottish and British was related to their ideas about language. It may be interesting to consider some studies carried out in Wales, a country where two languages are in use. Some children are monoglot English, some are monoglot Welsh, and between these two extremes are to be found various degrees of bilingualism. The whole problem of testing such a population has been studied by Jenkins (1962).

In the industrial districts of South Wales, English is the language most commonly used, with Welsh being taught as a second language. In this area, Jenkins found that the place where they had been born, rather than the language they spoke or their parents' nationalities, decided whether children thought themselves English or Welsh. Their attitudes to learning Welsh seemed to depend on whether their parents spoke it or not, according to Jones (1949, 1950).

Some areas where differences between bilingual and monoglot students seemed possible were the subject of an investigation by Davies (1957). Among students at a Welsh University College, he found that the monoglots tended to be more radical in their outlook than the bilinguals, but that there was no difference in the emotional sensitivity of the two groups. Their cultural attitudes and interests were also similar, but the bilinguals were, if anything, more creative generally and especially so in literature, music and crafts. No relationship was found between social status and cultural attitudes, but, among the bilingual students, a correlation of $+0.42$ was found between scores on a scale measuring their Welsh linguistic background and one measuring cultural attitudes.

It will be appreciated that the field of intergroup attitudes is a wide one. It includes not only international attitudes, about which most work has been done, but also attitudes between members of different social classes, which may have considerable effect on the harmonious conduct of national affairs. Within the local community, too, attitudes between members of different families may be important.

One of the aims of education in our time should be to try to reduce, rather than increase, tension between different groups and to promote friendly feelings within them. Most of us will have had the experience of finding that someone who, as a stranger, seemed unlikeable and forbidding, turned out on closer acquaintance to be a pleasant companion with interests and ideas very like our own. We also know that understanding other people's difficulties can often lead to greater tolerance of their peculiarities. The results of experiments with children show that their attitudes to foreigners can be modified in these ways, too.

A necessary step, then, towards international understanding is to give children, while they are still young, every chance to get to know and understand foreign peoples and their ways. But this alone is not enough. A child who is insecure himself is likely to see other people as a threat, no matter how well he knows them. To such a child, different means dangerous.

Thus if we wish to promote intergroup harmony, we must take into account a child's feeling about himself and his feeling for other members of his own group. Only when a child can accept himself as he is, and has a healthy relationship with those around him, can he be expected to accept easily members of other groups and not see strangers, whether they are foreigners or not, as a threat to himself and his own security. Attitude to the self, attitude to authority, and intergroup attitudes are all related, and all three must be taken into account in educating children to live at peace with their neighbours in the modern world. Enthusiasm for work on international attitudes should not be allowed to blind us to the importance of those other attitudes which are also fundamental and which may be more within the control of most schools.

VIII

INTERESTS: ORIGINS
AND DEVELOPMENT

SO FAR, we have been considering attitudes and their importance is obvious. It is easy, too, to see how the terms *attitude*
and *interest* can be confused, and why they are sometimes used
in ways which suggest that they are almost interchangeable.
Attitude is the broader term, and an attitude represents a
general orientation of the individual. Interest, on the other
hand, is more specific and is directed towards a particular
object or activity. It is a response of liking or attraction, and
Strong (1943) stresses that it is an aspect of behaviour and
not an entity in itself.

The question of how interests originate is of considerable
importance in education. In a class of boys, one likes making
model aeroplanes, another has no interest in practical hobbies
but enjoys trying to write stories, while a third, despising both
literary and practical pursuits, delights in spending as much
time as possible in the Youth Club with his own gang. Why
are their interests so different? Are interests biologically determined, the products of inherited factors, or are they the result
of the social and physical environment in which the individual
grows up ?

Attempts at answering this question have, in some cases,
involved studies of the interests of parents and children or of
fraternal and identical twins. Carter (1932) claimed to have
found definite family resemblances in occupational interests,
with those of identical twins being more alike than those of
fraternal twins. At the same time, the interests of fraternal
twins were positively correlated. He drew the conclusion that

Interests: Origins and Development

heredity was more important than environment in determining interests, but it was obvious that environment also had an effect. This is only to be expected, for children growing up in the same family are exposed to very similar opportunities for acquiring interests, and, quite apart from their inherited tendencies, it would be odd if they did not acquire the same ones to some extent.

The influence of family environment can be seen in the results obtained by Berdie (1943). He noted that the income and occupational status of fathers seemed to govern, to some extent, the interests of their sons. Technical interests predominated in the lower income groups, while business interests went with higher incomes in many cases.

It is not only the occupations of the parents that count, in this context, but also their own interests and hobbies. Lovell and White (1958) found that students choosing to study science were significantly more likely to have fathers who had scientific interests and who had tried to impart to their sons technical knowledge and skills. Meyer and Penfold (1961) added the observation that children's beliefs about their parents' interests mattered more than the actual interests, indicating that children tend to model themselves on their parents as they see them, whether the picture is accurate or not.

The wider environment, outside the family, also plays a part in determining interests, and Rallison (1939) found that town children developed a wider range of scientific interests, and at an earlier age, than country children. School, too, can be a major influence in developing interests which persist in later life. It would be discouraging if this were not the case, for it is at school that most people find their opportunities for sampling a wide range of academic and other pursuits and deciding which, if any, they wish to continue studying and using in after-school years.

Sometimes the choice is on the basis of achievement, and it is true that many people become interested in subjects they can do well, though neither this statement nor the converse should be made without an examination of the available evidence. Lovell and White (1958) found that success at, and a liking for, arithmetic during junior school years inclined students to choose to take science later, and Flood and Crosland (1947) found that the interest of University Extra-Mural and W.E.A. students in a subject often dated from their school days. Other influences arousing their interest were books, magazines, broadcasts, relatives, friends and films.

Environmental influences obviously play an important part in determining the interests which an individual develops. Heredity, on the other hand, may play a considerable part also, and may be the factor which determines the individual's success or failure at the activities suggested as possible interests by his social environment. The question of the relationship between interest and achievement is so important that it must be given a separate chapter, but it is arguable that a lack of success may well cause individuals to desist from following interests which they may find to hand in their environment, and may induce them to turn their attention to alternative occupations.

The observation made by Boynton (1940) that children who do not have a hobby often show a different and probably less desirable type of personality adjustment than was usually found in those who had hobbies may be relevant here. It is possible that adjustment may depend on innate endocrine characteristics, and there is evidence that interests are, to some extent related to adjustment. Darley (1938) found that men with primary interest patterns in technical occupations had poorer morale scores than men in all the other groups except verbal occupations. They had greater feelings of inferiority than men with interest in business or social contact, and had markedly poorer social adjustment and more limited social skills than most other groups. On the other hand, they tended to have good home, health and emotional adjustments. Men with social service interests tended to fall at the less masculine end of the Strong scale, but did not show characteristic adjustments in general. Business contact interests seemed to go with better social adjustments and greater social skill than was found with most other types of interest.

The question which immediately springs to mind is 'Which comes first?' Does the person with a particular type of adjustment or maladjustment develop interests which accord with it, or is the final level of adjustment the result of pursuing a particular kind of interest? Darley expressed the opinion that personality characteristics seem to be developmentally determined in individuals before they receive any occupational training, so that it would seem that the adjustment is primary and the type of interest shown depends on this. If this is really true, there is a strong case for the practice of considering personality as well as ability in vocational guidance. Similar results to Darley's were obtained by Berdie (1943).

It must be stressed that findings such as these are based on group averages and that wide variations were found in all groups. It would be a mistake, therefore, to make assumptions about the adjustment of individuals based only on a knowledge of their predominant interests. General conclusions should always be re-examined in the light of information obtained from individuals before they are made the basis for vocational guidance.

We have mentioned heredity and environment as possible factors conditioning the interests of individuals, but this is only part of the story. Interest is interest of a person in something, and so far only the person has been discussed. It is now time to turn to the objects of interest and attempt to discover what are the inherent qualities which make them interesting. Because this book is concerned with education, it seems fitting to devote the main part of this discussion to an examination of the interests of children and young people. Three spheres of interest seem likely to yield important information, and it is proposed to consider now the interests of pupils in what they learn at school, their hobbies or leisure interests, and their reading interests.

The interest shown by children in the subjects they learn

at school is an obvious and well-studied field of enquiry. Pritchard (1935) and Shakespeare (1936) reported typical results. Among pupils of all ages, the most popular subjects are usually those allowing plenty of activity, and opportunities for discussion, argument and the possibility of proving things for themselves make for interest. The dull lessons are the ones where the teacher does all the talking.

Two main types of interest have been noted, described as subjective, or interest in the process, as in mathematics, and objective, or interest in the subject matter, as in literary subjects. Objective interests usually rank higher than subjective ones. Stephenson (1936b), using inverted factor analysis, classified school subjects into scientific and linguistic and found a slight bias among pupils for scientific subjects. This is in line with the work mentioned above, for scientific subjects, at the school stage, are often the ones which give most scope for activity on the part of the pupils. Essentially similar results have been obtained by Lambert (1944) and Davies (1959).

Schools which allow children a free choice of activity during a part of the school day can provide a good deal of information about their interests. Hughes (1955) reported that in two junior schools the activities chosen by the children were rarely in the form of play or games. Indeed, these accounted for less than 10% of the activities chosen. Art and craft pursuits, drawing, painting and making things, were the most popular of all through the school, but literate pursuits were also popular and became more so as the children got older. These included reading, writing, arithmetic, acting, and discovery subjects involving finding out about countries and people, natural history and science. The very wide range of activities going on at any one time in a class, and also in those sampled at different times by individual children, was remarkable. It seems likely that junior school children will, given the chance, experiment with all kinds of occupations, and in this way they discover their own bents.

Among older children, a greater selectivity is to be expected, but the diversity of school hobbies clubs shows that their interests cover a wide range, too. Boys tend to have more varied interests than girls, and grammar school children than those in secondary modern schools, according to Stewart (1950).

What boys and girls do out of school is likely to be more revealing of their real interests than either what they do in school or their feelings about their lessons. The great diversity of children's leisure activities was brought out by an enquiry carried out by Stewart (1950) in Ilford. Sporting activities accounted for 61% of the leisure occupations of boys and 45% of those of girls. These were not by any means all competitive, especially in the case of the girls, and cycling and swimming ranked high in popularity. Passive sporting activities, such as watching matches, increased with age. Expressive activities, acting, writing and so forth, were more popular among girls than boys, and so were entertainments like the cinema and theatre.

Differences were noted between grammar and modern school pupils. Cricket and tennis were more popular in grammar schools and football in modern schools. Gardening, cooking, housework, the cinema and dancing were commoner interests in modern than grammar schools, while collecting tended to be a grammar school hobby. It is possible that some of these differences may really be social class or economic differences between pupils in the two types of schools.

Collecting is a popular hobby at all ages, but probably children of twelve or thirteen are the most avid collectors. Boys and girls collect different things, but both are interested in stamps. Boys also collect more than girls, possibly because they have more pockets in which to keep their acquisitions.

Stewart's findings should be compared with more recent results obtained by Curr, Hallworth and Wilkinson (1962). As part of a projected nation wide investigation into the leisure activities, interests and attitudes of school children, the boys and girls in a secondary modern school in Birmingham were asked to keep a detailed diary of their activities for three days, a Wednesday, a Saturday and a Sunday. Watching television turned out to be their chief waking occupation out of school hours, amounting to thirteen hours a week, on the average. Walking and talking with friends of their own age came next in importance for both boys and girls. Hobbies and books took little time and games less still. Girls spent a good deal of time on household chores, but boys got off lightly in that respect. Both sexes put in some time at paid work on Saturdays.

The most interesting point here is the dominance of television. When Stewart's enquiry was conducted, it was still a comparatively new medium, but in the intervening years it has become a commonplace, and the extent to which it occupies the leisure hours of school children is brought out by this Birmingham enquiry.

Children's reading interests have come in for a good deal of attention, and enquiries by Carsley (1957), Whitehead (1956), Stewart (1950) and Williams (1951) are typical. Most children seem to enjoy reading more at home than at school, but, at the same time, they often like listening to the teacher reading aloud. Both boys and girls usually like adventure and mystery stories, but where boys choose books on sport and encyclopaedias, girls tend to go for school and Biblical stories. Cowboy stories and fairy stories seem to rank low generally.

There is a considerable amount of non-fiction read by children, partly because they use books for information about their hobbies. It is in books of this kind that they appreciate illustrations. In fiction, many children dislike illustrations, though a good picture on the dust jacket often attracts them.

The appeal of so-called children's classics is anything but universal, and some children read and enjoy what are intended to be adult books. Even children who are more intellectually able than the average, though, have been found to enjoy books written in simple language and whose themes are relatively immature. Important ingredients are a hero or heroine with whom the readers can identify and a plot with a strong element of wish-fulfilment. There is a good case for giving children opportunities to choose their own reading from a very wide selection of books, and not merely from those usually considered suitable for their age.

Books account for only a small part of the reading of most children. Periodicals classed as comics and bloods are read in large numbers by both boys and girls well into the secondary school age range. Grammar school children seem to grow out of them earlier than children in secondary modern schools, and the ones they read are usually of better quality, probably because of their greater maturity and better powers of reading. Among older boys, sporting papers are always popular, and older girls tend to read women's magazines.

Newspaper reading often reflects the interests of the parents rather than of the children. The newspaper is in the home and the children read it, but they do not choose it as a rule. It is sometimes forgotten that a child who has learned to read tends to read anything that comes to hand, and this applies to notices and advertisements as well as to books, periodicals and news-papers. Often, on a journey, one hears a small child spelling out names of stations and names on luggage labels with interest as great as that it shows in its own comic. In an informal enquiry several years ago, lists of books children said they had read were found to contain an appreciable sprinkling of books of an earlier period, and it was a fair assumption that these had belonged to parents and grandparents and had been found at home and sampled by another generation of children. Certainly, many of them would not, at that date, have been on sale in any but a second-hand bookshop. What children read may be an indication of what is available to them as much as an indication of their choice. What they like and dis-like in what they read, tells us something about their own tastes.

More recent work on children's reading supplements and confirms, but does not supersede, that of Jenkinson (1940). In his opinion, most children would acquire the reading habit without any help from schools, and it is necessary for their tastes to pass through some natural stages of development. Much of the inferior literature they read from choice assists this process, and is chosen because it either promotes growing up or helps to compensate for the difficulties of doing so. A book is not only a source of information or entertainment, but also a form of escape, and this is true whatever the age of the reader. Children should not be denied the escape which is provided by their bloods and comics from the sometimes harsh world of reality, any more than their elders should be prevented from reading thrillers, archaeological works or space fiction.

There is a very strong case for helping children to build up the habit of reading. Books are still the major source of information available to most of us, and children who have learnt to turn to books for help and who know how to use them are on the way to getting a good education. The first stage is reading for fun, and the earlier children discover the joys of reading the better. They are more likely to do this if they have parents who read for pleasure and if there are books lying about or in bookcases at home. Children tend to do what they see adults doing, and if their parents never read, then the children are likely to regard reading as something done at school rather than as an adult occupation or pleasure. Outside and after school, they will then tend not to read, and so their education will be stunted. Indeed, under such circumstances, it is quite possible for a child who has learnt to read at school, but found it difficult, to forget the art and to become illiterate in quite a short time.

How many of the interests enjoyed and developed during schooldays survive into after-school life? Some do, and some lead on to careers where they can be used. Scientific or craft interests are examples which spring to mind. But many will be left behind when the doors of the school close for the last time on the boys and girls who have pursued them there. 'Now I am become a man and I put away childish things' represents one attitude, but sometimes interests may be abandoned with regret, because facilities that were available at school are not present at home, or because work or further study leaves little free time.

Interests: Origins and Development

Growing out of one set of interests would not matter as long as others took their place, but Veness (1962) found that boys and girls nearing school leaving age had few ideas about new things they wanted to do. Games, the cinema and other passive amusements ranked high in their plans. Some, especially grammar school children, hoped to spend more time on gardening and other constructive hobbies. Reading and hobbies of the study type were expected to be maintained, and boys hoped to pursue scientific interests.

As might be expected, social interests were especially marked out as increasing after schooldays, but it was the informal activities, rather than organised and uniformed movements, that were going to be important. This corresponds with information about their own interests obtained from Youth Club members, most of whom had left school. (Evans, 1960.) Activities at the club took up a great deal of their spare time, but only 2 or 3% mentioned belonging to movements like the A.T.C., Scouts, or St. John Ambulance Brigade. Going out with friends, either of their own sex or the opposite one, was the commonest occupation mentioned for the evenings. Some went dancing or to the cinema, especially at weekends. A very small minority engaged in games or other athletic activities such as hiking, skating, swimming and cycling. A few went to evening classes, concerts and jazz clubs or took part in discussion groups or amateur dramatics. On Sundays some visited relations or went to church.

The general impression was that, while taken as whole, the group could produce a fairly wide range of quite unexceptionable activities, what any one member did tended to conform to a set and restricted pattern. There were a few enthusiasts for each of the activities mentioned, but their appeal was limited to those few. The kind of experimentation which should be part of the process of growing up did not seem to be going on, and Veness recorded the same impression of a lack of ideas among her subjects.

It has been noted by Chisnall (1942) and Hammond (1945) that there are really only two types of activity pursued by young people, athletic and sedentary, and that intellectual and individual interests are much less popular than active social ones. Why does the eager interest in all kinds of activities shown by junior school children give way, before they are grown up, to inertia and lack of initiative in so many cases? This is a question which educationists ought to ponder, and, if the fault is in our teaching, we should attempt to remedy the defect. It may be that the kinds of interests we encourage at school are too far from those of the out-of-school world of the children to have much chance of survival. Idealism must be tinged with realism if it is to accomplish its aims.

IX

INTEREST QUESTIONNAIRES

THE LAST CHAPTER illustrates the very wide range of activities in which boys and girls may be interested. What their specific interests may be depends to a great extent on the circumstances of their individual lives, but some classification of these interests is necessary if they are to be taken into account in educational or vocational guidance. Interest questionnaires used in this work attempt to build up a picture of interest in wide fields from information about interest in particular objects or activities.

Interests have been classified in many ways. Fryer (1931) suggested two classes, subjective and objective. Super (1949) carried the differentiation further and distinguished four main types of interest, which he called expressed, manifest, tested and inventoried.

A number of factor-analytical studies of the results of interest inventories have been made with a view to determining basic interest factors. Indeed, Thurstone's first application of his new method of factor analysis was to a list of intercorrelations of the interests of eighteen professions supplied by Strong. (Thurstone, 1931.) This resulted in the extraction of four factors which it was necessary to postulate in order to account for the given table of correlations, and these, after inspection of the loadings in these factors for the eighteen professions, were named interest in science, interest in language, interest in people and interest in business. Although he admitted that there are probably other factors of minor significance or of significance in a relatively small number of instances, Thurstone asserted that it should be possible to construct profiles of professional interests for individuals on the basis of scores in these four factors. Support for this theory soon came from Carter, Pyles and Bretnall (1935) and Ferguson, Humphreys and Strong (1941).

The movement, once started, progressed, and studies of this type multiplied. Their authors did not always use the same tests or the same techniques and their terminology varied, but Super (1949) found, on examining the results presented by a number of writers, that there was considerable agreement about two of Thurstone's factors. The first was alternatively called theoretical or scientific, but it obviously corresponded to an interest in understanding the why and how of things. The second, which Thurstone called interest in people, was sometimes called social, social-service or social-welfare, but it represented an interest in people for their own sakes. Super has presented the results of his investigations in the form of a synthesis of several existing studies and suggested eight independent interest factors, scientific, social-welfare, literary, material, systematic or record-keeping, contact, artistic and musical.

A classification of high-grade occupational interests presented by Vernon (1949) presents a different approach. Fifty-eight high-grade occupations were classified, using the method of paired comparisons, on the basis of their similarities and differences, and the results were factor analysed. Four factors were identified.

1. Gregarious *vs.* Isolated.
2. Social welfare *vs.* Administration.
3. Scientific *vs.* Display.
4. Verbal *vs.* Active.

There is no mention of artistic and aesthetic factors, since these were not clear in the analysis, and the religious factor was not confirmed, possibly because very few of the items used were concerned with spiritual ideals. Factor analysis cannot produce information that has not first been introduced into the test material, whether this is done by accident or design, and this should be kept in mind when results such as those mentioned in this chapter are being assessed.

In view of the amount of research which has been carried out on interests, it is surprising to find that methods of assessment have not advanced perceptibly from those noted by Fryer in 1931. In his pioneer volume on the subject, he mentioned that, at that date, interests had only recently been made the subject of psychological measurement, and he compared the work being done then with that being done on the measurement of abilities in the early years of this century. He prophesied that the subjective measures of interest then in use would be superseded by objective measures, except in so far as they contributed something additional to the measurement.

Using his two proposed categories of interest, subjective and objective, Fryer considered various methods of assessment. Subjective interests were studied mainly by the use of inventories, of which Strong's was the most important. The principle was that individuals estimated the strength of their own feelings and supplied subjective assessments. The scoring might be objective, but the responses scored were not.

These inventories might be concerned with universal interests or the interests of defined groups of people, such as vocational groups. Fryer criticised early inventories because of errors of sampling, saying that the items included had not been systematically selected and that later inventories were based on earlier ones. Items were added or discarded according as they did or did not distinguish between groups, and the end result was a collection of distinguishing interests, which might separate out the members of some groups but not those of others whose interests were not included. Inventories of this kind give no information about interests which cut across all group boundaries and are held by many types of people. In this type of study, indifference may be as important as interest or aversion.

Objective measures of interest mentioned by Fryer are the

information test and the free association test. The information test deals with a specialised field, and in examining the interests of an individual a whole series of such tests may have to be applied, each dealing with a separate field of possible interest. The free association test has the advantage that one test can be scored for responses in a variety of fields, and is thus more economical of time and effort than the information test.

The remainder of this chapter is taken up with descriptions of a number of questionnaires which have been used in the assessment of interests. This work is included for the benefit of readers who may require information about their construction and usefulness, and it can be omitted by those who do not need such information and who prefer to pass on to the following, and less technical, chapters.

It will be appreciated that a very large number of instruments of this kind have been constructed, and it would be quite impossible to list them all, so a selection is given. The choice has been made with the aim of illustrating different methods of interest assessment, and in this respect no two of the tests described are identical. Two are American in origin and three are British. All were constructed as aids in vocational guidance. The Allport-Vernon *Study of Values* might have been included here, but it has already been mentioned in an earlier chapter, and it deals with evaluative attitudes rather than with interests.

The Strong Vocational Interest Blank

This test has been the subject of a great deal of research and much of the early work has been described by Strong (1943). The underlying assumption is that men and women engaged in a particular occupation have characteristic likes and dislikes, and that they resemble one another more in these than they resemble people in other occupations. After much experimentation, Strong claimed to have identified patterns of interest which differentiated members of a number of occupational groups, and the *Vocational Interest Blank* is a device for determining an individual's interests and comparing his pattern with those of these occupational groups.

It was recognised that likenesses among individuals are more obvious than differences between them, and that there are many interests which are common to very large numbers of people in many occupations. Knowledge of interests like these is of no great use in vocational guidance, so Strong and his associates set out to discover any interests or patterns of interest which served to contrast men in a particular occupation with men-in-general. This emphasis on differential interests is their great contribution to the theory of interest assessment. The score of an individual on the *Blank* is an estimate of the extent to which his interests correspond with the differential interests of the occupation under consideration. The basic assumptions are that the interests of occupational groups can be differentiated in this way and that individuals can be matched with occupational groups on the basis of their interest scores.

Three further assumptions should be mentioned here. The first is that interests, once developed, are fairly permanent. It is obvious that it would be disastrous to base vocational guidance on transient phenomena, since a vocation is usually chosen for a long period, if not always for life. Strong found that the interests of men changed very little between the ages of twenty-five and fifty-five, and that there was little change between twenty and twenty-five. Between fifteen and twenty, however, changes might be considerable, and he advocated that his test should not be used with boys below the age of seventeen.

The second assumption is that interests are not influenced to any great extent by vocational training and experience. If they are so influenced, the interests of occupational groups might be the results of training and experience in the occupation and it would be unrealistic to pick untrained and inexperienced recruits on the basis of interests which might change considerably as a result of a period at the work, or which might develop only because of experience of it.

Thirdly, there is the assumption that a young man or woman with interests corresponding to those of an occupational group will enjoy doing the work which men or women in that occupation do. It will be noted that the word is 'enjoy.' There is no mention of success, and Strong makes it quite plain in the manual that his *Blank* is not meant to indicate the probable success of subjects selected by its means. Measures of ability, motivation and character are needed for this, while measures of interest contribute information of the probable satisfaction and happiness of the candidates.

There are separate *Vocational Interest Blanks* for men and women, and each contains 400 items, of which 263 appear in both forms. The original *Blank* was published in 1927, and could be scored for thirty-nine occupations for men and eighteen for women. In the 1959 version, forty-eight scales for men and twenty-nine for women are available. Scoring is extremely complicated and time-consuming and is best carried out by machine. For this reason, it is unusual to find all the scales being used, and it is common practice to score only a selection for any individual being tested, though Strong deprecates this.

The test was standardised by reference to the interests of men and women known to be successful in their occupations, and Strong (1959) has given details of the groups used. He gives split-half reliabilities ranging from 0·76 to 0·94 for seventeen of the men's scales, while test-retest reliabilities over an eighteen-year period for the same scales range from 0·48 to 0·79.

In addition to data about the occupations listed, the *Blank* gives measures of occupational level, specialisation level, interest maturity and masculinity-femininity.

The Kuder Preference Record

Like the *Strong Vocational Interest Blank*, this is the result of considerable experimentation. The first form was published in 1939, and since then many refinements have been introduced, based on the findings of continual research financed by part of the income from the sale of the test.

The aim of the *Preference Record* is to discover what the subject likes to do and what he does not like to do, and to match his preferences with activities connected with vocations. This is done by presenting him with 168 sets of activities, with three in each set, and directing him to indicate which in each set he likes most and least. This enables his preferences for the three activities to be put in order and paired comparisons between them can be made. One of the triads reads:

> Tinker with a broken sewing machine.
> Play a piano.
> Sketch an interesting scene.

The format of the test is ingenious and usually arouses interest. The subject has to indicate his likes and dislikes by pricking through an answer pad with a pin. The pricks are registered on a record sheet and are counted to obtain an estimate of interest in ten different fields. In contrast to the *Strong Vocational Interest Blank*, the scoring is rapid and easy and can be done by the subjects themselves. A profile of interests is then drawn, and the relative strengths and weaknesses in different fields of interest can be studied.

The major fields of interest for which preferences can be obtained are outdoor, mechanical, computational, scientific, persuasive, artistic, literary, musical, social service and clerical. A verification, or V, scale is also included, which serves to check the accuracy with which the instructions have been followed. It works on the principle that there are some interests which are so common that they are recorded by nearly everyone, and the V scale takes note of these. Subjects who record very few of these interests are considered likely to have responded carelessly or insincerely, and a check can be made. It is always possible, of course, that the check may disclose a really unusual interest pattern, but it is more likely to point to mistakes in answering which can then be corrected. It is important that guidance should be based on accurate information about interests, and the V scale helps to ensure accuracy.

The manual to the *Record* contains a long list of occupations, classified under the ten categories of interest, and divided up according to various levels from professional to semi-skilled. Indications are also given of the kind of work involved, in terms of individual preferences. In this way it is possible to take into account such factors as preference for being active in groups, for familiar and stable situations, for working with ideas, for avoiding conflict and for directing and influencing others.

Reliabilities for the *Record* reported by Kuder (1956) range from 0·84 to 0·92. These were obtained for the separate scales by studying the preferences of 1000 men, 100 women, 100 boys and 100 girls. Profile scores for the occupational groups were obtained from over 15,000 students.

In spite of the vast amount of work which has been done on it, it does appear that the *Preference Record* is open to faking, and its use should be restricted to situations where the subjects appreciate the need for truthfulness and wish to co-operate. A test which is of little use when promotion depends on the result, may be a very useful instrument where vocational guidance is desired. The *Record* is also of much less use in Britain than in the United States, since both vocabulary and norms relate to the latter country. This is true of the *Strong Vocational Interest Blank*, too.

The Lambert and Peel General Information Test

Unlike the Strong and Kuder questionnaires, the Lambert and Peel *General Information Test* is designed for a restricted age range and a limited task. It was designed to identify the interests of children in only two fields, the practical and the academic, at around the age of transfer to secondary education. Essentially, it is an information test, interest being assessed by the knowledge which has been acquired about the topic of interest.

Interest Questionnaires

It was recognised that the more able children are likely to have amassed a considerable amount of information on most topics, irrespective of their true interests, and that a test of information was at least as likely to measure intelligence as interest. To get over this difficulty, an element of choice has been introduced into the test. Items are arranged six to a page, and the subjects instructed to answer only three. The items are equally divided between practical and academic topics, so that a child may answer three of one type or two of one type and one of the other, the argument being that he will choose items in line with his interests. The information called for is such as a child might acquire outside school, rather than during formal education.

Because it was found that there was a tendency to answer earlier questions on a page in the easier sub-tests, a second part was constructed. This was really a vocabulary test, the words being arranged in sets of six and meanings of three from each set being required. Again the scheme of three practical and three academic items per set was adhered to, but, in this case, the small number of words could be taken in at a glance, and it was thought that this would be conducive to a real choice being made instead of the first three seen being attempted.

Two scores can be obtained for each subject, one for practical items (P) and the other for academic items (A). The difference between these, $(P - A)$, is taken as an assessment of practical interests. To get over the difficulty caused by children of greater ability being able to answer more questions than less able children, the expression $100\ (P - A)/(P + A)$ is sometimes used as a measure of practical interest. The factor 100 is introduced to avoid fractional scores.

Peel (1948) correlated practical scores on the test with scores on the *Alexander Performance Scale* and obtained coefficients of $+0.2490$ and $+0.2332$. The correlation with the *Moray House Intelligence Test* was -0.2609. The subjects were 173 boys, aged $11+$.

This test was developed as a result of earlier work on

interest as a basis for secondary school selection by Lambert (1949).

The Wiseman and Fitzpatrick Devon Interest Test

Like the Lambert and Peel *General Information Test*, the *Devon Interest Test* was constructed to aid in the selection for technical education of boys and girls aged 11+ to 13+. No attempt is made to obtain a detailed picture of the children's interests, but only to assess the relative strengths of their interests in the two broad fields designated academic and practical. Two separate scores, an A-score (academic) and a P-score (practical) are obtained for each child.

The method is to ask the children to say whether they like or dislike various activities, or whether they 'don't know.' The activities are arranged in 'boxes', six to a box, and in each group the children have also to mark those they like best and second best. Each box contains two practical and two academic activities, and the other two are neutral in these respects. Neutral activities include such items as playing football, playing with other children, eating sweets and ice-cream and going to the circus. These distractors were found to be valuable, in that a child who chose a practical item rather than a strong distractor was likely to have a real interest in practical occupations. (Fitzpatrick and Wiseman, 1954.)

Experiments with a sample of 600 children in Cornish schools showed that the test differentiated at the 1% level of significance between children aged 13+ in the three types of schools, grammar, central and secondary modern. For the girls, only the P-score differences were significant, but both the A-score and P-score differences were significant for the boys. Reliabilities for this sample were for boys, 0·91 for P-scores and 0·88 for A-scores, and for girls, 0·90 and 0·88 respectively.

Correlations of P-scores with a number of assessments of intelligence and attainment in English and arithmetic have been found to be negligible, but the correlation with scores derived from school report forms covering, among other things, teachers' estimates of technical ability, interest and ability in practical subjects, strongest and weakest school subjects and vocational ambition was reported to be +0·246. Correlations between P- and A-scores were given as –0·66 for boys and –0·36 for girls, showing that the two types of interest assessed by the test are independent of one another. Factor analysis suggested that P-scores are similar to technical scores in structure.

A further experiment with 175 boys, aged 11+, has been reported. (Wiseman, 1955.) The results obtained were similar to those for children of 13+, and in this case a comparison was made with the Lambert and Peel test. Correlation between the P-scores on the two tests was found to be negligible (–0·087), and the *Devon Test* was reported to be more heavily loaded in the interest factor than the Lambert and Peel test. Both the *Devon Interest Test* and the Lambert and Peel *General Information Test* have been used in the programmes of the National Foundation for Educational Research. With two small samples of boys and girls from single-sex technical schools, it was found that at age eleven the *General Information Test* showed higher academic than practical scores for both sexes. The *Devon Interest Test* produced the opposite result. Wiegersma and Barr (1959) considered that this was to be expected because of the different natures of the tests. Because of the bias of most primary school courses, academic knowledge is likely to be greater than practical knowledge at this age, but the real preferences of most children are for practical activities. The conclusion is that, at this age, the *Devon Test* may be a more successful measure of interest than the Lambert and Peel test. Both tests bring out the greater practical interests of boys as opposed to girls, while their academic interests are very much the same.

The Fleming Cotswold Personality Assessment (P.A. I)

This test differs from those already described in some im-

113

portant particulars. To begin with, it includes both questionnaires on preferences and a set of modified Likert-type attitude scales. The preferences are classed under three broad categories, ideas, people and things, and in this it resembles the *General Information* and *Devon* tests rather than the Strong and Kuder tests. It differs from the two former tests in that it includes an assessment of social as well as practical and academic interests, and for this reason it is of use in the study of personality as well as in educational guidance. It is designed for use with members of youth clubs and with boys and girls at school.

Of the nine subjects, the first five are measures of interests. The first, headed *Knowing Your Own Mind*, calls for a numerical assessment of agreement with each of a set of twelve statements, such as:

Tom said he liked best doing things with his hands.

Mabel said she would rather read a story.

Sam said he would rather learn to dance.

The remaining interest sub-tests are headed *Talking About Wishes, Judging Other People, Choosing Work* and *Spending Money*. They contain, in all, sixty-six items, twenty-two referring to each of the three types of interest. By summing the votes given, interest profiles can be obtained showing the relative strengths of the three types of interest.

There is evidence (Fleming, Digaria and Newth, 1960) that the three types of interest are relatively independent and that the patterns obtained by factorial analysis for boys and girls are comparable. Long-term studies suggest that interests as measured by this test remain only moderately stable during the secondary school years.

The interest questionnaires were validated by considering the scores made by about 1000 pupils in relation to the results of selection tests at the age of $13+$, to the opinions of their teachers, and by the use of case studies. Repeat reliabilities after the interval of a month for one hundred pupils were found to be $+0.84$ (things), $+0.90$ (people) and $+0.81$ (ideas).

Interest Questionnaires

The three attitude scales are entitled *Using One's Hands*, *Being With Other People* and *Talking About School*, and are concerned with practical activities, social relationships and schooling. They thus correspond with the three types of interest assessed in the earlier part of the test. Test-retest reliabilities for the first two after an interval of a month were $+0.87$ and $+0.85$, and for the last, after a week's interval, $+0.93$.

The last part of the test is headed *Keeping A Record* and is a list, in three columns, of leisure activities, practical, social and intellectual. The subjects have to check any they have done in the last two weeks and any they wish they had done. No score is obtained from this, but the information can be used in conjunction with the results of the other tests.

Use of the test in selection at 13+ for technical, commercial and art schools was followed up, and the results correlated with later school success. Coefficients of the order of $+0.3$ were obtained with small groups of boys and girls taking subjects such as engineering drawing, art, book-keeping and shorthand.

It is interesting to look at these tests in the light of hopes for progress in interest assessment expressed by Fryer (1931). Strong and Kuder both used inventories of the type with which Fryer was familiar. Lambert and Peel used an information test, and also introduced an element of free association when they asked for a choice to be made among the questions to be answered. The *Devon Interest Test* and the *Cotswold Personality Assessment* (*P.A. 1*) are both what Fryer would have called subjective measures. The theory of interest assessment appears to be very much as it was in 1931, and any advances which have been made seem to be in techniques of applying it or in the evaluation of results.

X

ATTITUDES, INTERESTS
AND ACHIEVEMENT

THE USE OF INFORMATION about interests in vocational and educational guidance is based on the assumption, widely held, that interest and ability go together. 'If you really want to do a thing, there is a fair chance that you will be successful at it.' It is also believed that success is unlikely where interest is lacking. At the same time, our system of educational guidance in England and Wales has, for many years, been based on assessments of ability and achievement, and the allocation of children to secondary schools has proceeded without any real enquiry about the interests of individual children, in spite of the division into types outlined in the Norwood Report of 1941. A bookish child of I.Q. 100 is likely to end up in a secondary modern school, while his friend of I.Q. 120, with exclusively practical interests, will most probably find his way into a grammar school. The spread of comprehensive education may help to check anomalies of this kind, occurring when selection is based almost entirely on academic ability and achievement. At later stages, the likes and dislikes of pupils come into the picture. Pupils choose the subjects they wish to take for public examinations partly because they like them, and a school which attempted a severe division of pupils on ability alone might be the target for considerable criticism. The belief that people have the right to do what they want to do, dies hard, and children as well as their parents do not usually want to do only what teachers say they can do.

Where further education is concerned, entry to courses is open to students who have the requisite preliminary qualifications, and their choice of course, subject to being qualified, is based on personal factors of which interest is usually one of the more important. It is unusual, though for more than a cursory enquiry about interests to be made, the application for a particular course being assumed to be an indication of a real desire to follow it.

More attention is given to interests in the case of vocational guidance, and this has begun to spread to educational guidance when technical as well as academic courses are involved. Tests of interest are most often attempts at distinguishing pupils whose interests are predominantly practical from those whose interests are more academic. Guidance of this kind, based on interests, can be made with confidence only if interests are constant, and it is important that children should not be guided into specialised courses of education until their interests have become stable.

The belief that general ability can be assessed at a much earlier age than interests or specialised abilities accounts for its almost exclusive use in educational guidance. Whether this belief is well founded is a point on which authorities disagree. Burt (1947) held that it is, but Peel (1949) seems more doubtful.

One of the main problems encountered in the allocation of children to different types of secondary school is that there is a significant correlation between academic and practical ability, and no clear division can be made on the basis of ability alone. The possibility that a test of academic and practical interests in conjunction with tests of ability might reduce the size of the group about whom no decision could be made was investigated by Lambert (1949) and Wiseman (1955). Both found that, even with the extra information obtained, there were still about 40% of the children who showed no significant bias either of ability or of interest. Though tests of interest give useful information, they do not come anywhere near providing a complete solution of the problem of secondary school guidance.

Even if a clear-cut division could be made at this age, it is doubtful whether it would be desirable. Unless there is definite evidence that interests have become stable by the age of eleven, the use of interest tests could result in wrong allocations just as surely as any other method. This is underlined by a further development of Lambert's work. When some boys who had been tested at 11+ were again tested after one or two years in secondary schools, a significant change in bias of interest was found, and in both grammar and modern schools this was away from the academic and towards the technical side of the curriculum. A wider curriculum, with more experience of practical subjects than they had enjoyed before the age of transfer, was held to be responsible for this shift of interest. This gives ground for warning against a too early decision, either by the children and their parents or by administrators, on the type of course to be followed.

Changes in bias of interest during the secondary school years have been noted by Fleming, Digaria and Newth (1960) also. The test used in their enquiries was Fleming's *P.A. 1.*, measuring interest in ideas, people and things. Long-term studies of pupils in boys' and girls' grammar schools showed that while interest in people remained relatively constant, interest in things dropped significantly between entry to the school and the age of about sixteen. Among girls, there was at the same time an increasing interest in ideas, but this was not noted among boys. A large cross-sectional study in secondary schools showed the same drop in interest in things among their pupils, while interest in people and ideas remained more or less stable. Possibly the difference between these results and that reported by Lambert is the consequence of the different types of test used. Where Lambert based assessments of interest on information, Fleming, Digaria and Newth were using a test of preferences, and while the second is claimed to be comparatively independent of mental ability, the former, because it depends on the acquisition of knowledge, is not. It is likely that *P.A. 1.* is a purer test of interest than either the *Devon Test* or the Lambert-Peel test. At the same time, it is probably more open to faking of responses than either of the others.

Attitudes, Interests and Achievement

If interest is to be considered as a factor in selection procedures, it is important to know whether it is related to subsequent success. Early studies by Dashiell (1919) and Bridges and Dollinger (1920) suggest that the correlation is low, though Thorndike (1921) produced more hopeful results. Part of the difficulty seems to be that measures of achievement may also be measures of application, and so assess interest to some extent. According to Berdie (1944), studies of interests are really studies of motivation, and both ability and interest must be taken into account when attempting to predict vocational success. Certainly, a good many people are likely to be wrongly placed in the occupations they would choose if left to themselves. Both Fryer (1923) and Stephen (1938) found that liking for work of a particular type did not seem to be related to intelligence at any age, and Harris (1949) thought that, at least in the case of Army Officers, the effects of training and interest might be more important than special aptitudes in ensuring success.

Among the reasons for the choice of a particular career, social conformity ranks high. There are fashions in occupations, as well as in hair styles, among young people of all social and educational levels. Vernon (1937 and 1938) found evidence of this among women university students and Macfarlane (1950) reported a similar state of affairs among secondary school children. Choice of career is influenced by the socio-economic status of the home, the range of local employment, tradition and fashion, as well as by experience of school subjects which can lead directly to a career.

Crazes are common during the secondary school years, but they can be dangerous when they influence work preferences. It is not enough to anticipate liking a job, unless there is also real knowledge of what it involves, and Williams (1962) found, like Macfarlane, that secondary school children often have very inaccurate ideas of this. A survey by Wiegersma and Barr (1959) confirmed that this is not at all an uncommon state of affairs. For this reason, it is important that any guidance, educational or vocational, should not be based on expressions of interest without making sure that these are founded on accurate information.

Some employers, nowadays, invite boys and girls approaching school leaving age to spend a little time in their factories before they actually start work, and this is a good move, from the point of view of both employer and potential employee. In some cases, it may save a good deal of trouble later. The boy who has set his heart on a particular kind of work, and who then finds himself unsuited to it, is in danger of beginning to drift from job to job, and may end as a pathetic misfit.

Usually, educational and vocational success are found to be related to intelligence more closely than to interest. The relationship between interest and intelligence is not a simple one, and there seems a possibility that some types of interest are more closely related to intelligence than others. Work by Carter (1932), Berdie (1943) and Davies (1959) supports this view. Interest in subjects like science and languages depends more on intelligence than do social interests, which are widespread among people of all intellectual levels. Where concentration and self-discipline are needed for success, as in reading or learning to play a musical instrument, Davies found that children of lower intelligence tended to lose interest sooner than more able children. Success in an interest can often lead to an improvement in school work, by boosting a child's morale and making effort seem worthwhile.

Intelligence sometimes determines the level at which an interest may function rather than the choice of interest. Stamp collecting, for example, may mean putting stamps in the right places in an album or it may become a highly specialised study of history, geography and the techniques of stamp production. Boynton (1940) found that superior intelligence seemed, among children of about eleven, to be associated with more diverse hobby interests, though no particular hobby was consistently associated with low intelligence. It is more important to know how an interest is expressed than to know of its existence when guidance is involved.

A combination of intelligence and interest may give a good

prognostication of success, but their relative importance should be taken into account. Angus (1950), using factor analysis, showed that interest in the subject played a much smaller part in success in science than intelligence, but he obtained a better prediction of the achievement of school children from a combination of measures of intelligence and interest than either gave on its own.

When considering interest and achievement in school subjects a number of factors must be taken into account. For one thing, the pleasure of succeeding may very well influence a child's liking for a subject, and Shakespeare (1936) found that among boys and girls at about the age of eleven there was a marked devotion to those subjects where results could be seen. They liked arithmetic and science, poetry and recitation, rather than literature, history and geography. Later, when they got nearer school leaving age, the utility subjects counted more. Pritchard (1935) also found that among pupils in forty-seven schools proficiency was one of the most frequent reasons given for liking a subject and failure at it for dislike.

It is possible that the effects of interest on achievement may be apparent in the long, rather than the short, term. Meyer and Penfold (1961) suggested that, in the early stages, interest may not necessarily be accompanied by good attainment. It may, nevertheless, result in continued effort which, eventually, brings success. If this is so, early success, resulting from ability, may give rise to interest, which in turn leads to persistent effort, and this combined with ability is likely to culminate in success.

It is possible, too, that interest contributes more to success in some fields than in others. Strong (1943) noted that likenesses among the interests of individuals are more striking than differences, and that age, sex and economic and occupational status do not seem to affect this. This overlapping in the interests of groups is an indication that no general relationship between interest and ability is to be expected. If there is a relationship, it is more likely to be found in specialised fields, not in those in which most people are interested, and this is borne out by evidence that scientific, mathematical and engineering interests are sometimes found related to ability, whereas social and business interests are not. Social interests are probably much more evenly spread throughout the population than are intellectual ones.

Another reason why interest and ability do not necessarily go together is that interest may be in unimportant details rather than in essentials. Rather dull children, whose teacher knows how to create a happy working atmosphere, may be interested in and enjoy arithmetic lessons at their own level of competence, but their scores on a standardised test of arithmetic would not correlate highly with this interest. Interest is geared to satisfaction rather than to success, and satisfaction may result from many causes, not all of which are related to success.

Neither is lack of interest necessarily related to failure. A man may spend his days working at a job which does not interest him greatly, or which he actually dislikes, but which gives him security and leisure in which to follow his real interests. Provided he has the necessary ability and is a conscientious worker, he is likely to be a satisfactory employee, though he might be happier if he were more deeply involved. There is satisfaction for many people in a job well done, no matter what the job is.

So far we have been considering interests in relation to achievement. Attitudes, which are more deeply rooted, as a rule, than interests, may also be expected to have some effect on success, and this has been found to be the case. Duffy and Crissy (1940) found low but statistically significant correlations between scores on related sections of the Allport-Vernon *Study of Values* and the Strong *Vocational Interest Bank*. For example, interest in the law as a career was positively related to economic and political values and negatively to aesthetic and religious ones, while positive aesthetic and negative economic values were associated with artistic and literary interests. It was suggested that high correlations were unlikely at the student stage, since vocational interests would still be only embryonic, while evaluative attitudes would be broader and better developed. If Carter (1940) is right in regarding development of vocational interests as being in the nature of an adjustment to environmental and personal conditions, then attitudes are very likely to affect them. Not only must home environment, needs, available cultural resources, physical and mental equipment be considered, but also the desire to identify with an admired group, and what is admired will depend on the individual's personal values. Identification leads to narrowing of experience and to greater knowledge of a particular vocational group in which interest is aroused. The vocational interests thus aroused become identified with the self, and attempts at identification with the admired pattern are made. If this proves too difficult, or the pattern is not satisfying enough, then another identification is attempted, and this goes on until a workable pattern is found. In this way, the growth of vocational interests is seen as part of the process of maturation, and support for the view is found in the observation that dull persons are frequently retarded in the development of vocational interests.

Some attitudes seem to be characteristic of particular levels of ability, and Duffy and Crissy (1940) noted that good students were more likely than poor ones to have high theoretical and aesthetic and low political and economic scores. Rigid stereotyped attitudes, too, can affect achievement in subjects where flexibility of outlook is necessary. It was found by Egner and Obelsky (1957) that, while students with stereotyped attitudes did well in mathematics and natural sciences, they did less well in the humanities and social sciences.

A certain amount of work has been done on the attitudes of school children towards school subjects, and generally the correlations between attitude scores and attainment have been low. Coefficients reported by Jordan (1937) ranged from $+0.21$ for English and geography to $+0.33$ for mathematics. Similar work was carried out by Stacey (1948) and Smith (1958).

It is possible that attitudes may be more important in some subjects than others, and Biggs (1959) quoted results in studies carried out for the National Foundation for Educational Research which suggest that attitude may be more closely related to success in arithmetic than it is to success in English. In general, there seemed to be evidence that poor attitudes were an important factor in failure in arithmetic, and that there were extreme cases where children developed a real fear of work involving numbers which could have a catastrophic effect on their progress in mathematics. Disliking English might not preclude success in that subject, but dislike of arithmetic was very likely to be accompanied by failure. Baraheni (1962) has produced results which appear to support this difference between the two subjects.

There seems to be a complex relationship between children's attitudes and their achievement at school. Arvidson (1956) thought that, although a better attitude to school was associated with higher marks, it was not the cause of them, but that attitude conditioned other factors which determined the child's achievement. For example, a good teacher may improve a child's attitude as well as its work, and a class that is favourably inclined may call out a teacher's best efforts on its behalf. Home conditions, too, may affect both attitude and achievement. Learning may be a challenge which will enhance the attitudes of the brighter children but discourage the less able, so that intelligence may be related to both attitude and achievement. Where intelligence, home and teacher all act in the same direction, the correlation between attitude and achievement is likely to be high, but one is not necessarily the fundamental cause of the other. The danger of regarding correlation between variables as evidence of a cause and effect relationship should not be overlooked in this or any other case.

This is in line with Glassey's (1945) finding that the attitudes of children and their parents to education are significantly correlated. Favourable attitudes did not necessarily lead to interest, though, for while the majority of children agreed that education was important and useful, many were only moderately interested in their school work because of methods used, the system and the teachers.

Attitudes, Interests and Achievement

It seems probable that neither interest nor attitudes are very closely related to success either in school subjects or in a vocation, and that general and special abilities are more important. If information about interests is to be used in guidance, it should be broadly based, concerned with a bias towards a group of subjects or occupations rather than to one in particular. Interest is likely to develop and change as a result of following a particular course of education or training, and its final expression may differ considerably in detail from its original form. Where attitudes are concerned, too, general ones may be most important. Values held, attitudes to the self, to authority and to work may affect success more than attitudes to school subjects or particular occupations. If considerations such as these are kept in mind, then knowledge of interests and attitudes may usefully supplement information about abilities and achievement in vocational and educational guidance.

XI

ATTITUDES, INTERESTS
AND TEACHING

NO BOOK ON EDUCATION is complete which deals only with the pupils, so this chapter begins with a discussion of the attitudes and interests of teachers. Not that teachers can be identified by their attitudes and interests or are markedly different from other professional people in these respects. Indeed, Strong found that he could not establish a scale of vocational interests for teachers in general, and this is only what one would expect. There is no reason why the teacher of science and the teacher of literature should be much more alike in their interests than are the scientist and the novelist, and it is likely that the interests of the teacher of science will resemble those of the scientist more closely than they do those of the teacher of literature.

Following on the last chapter, it may be useful to begin by considering the extent to which attitudes towards and interest in teaching are linked with teaching ability. There are a number of studies available which report correlations between scores on attitude scales and various measures of the efficiency of the teacher. One of the best known of these attitude scales was drawn up by Yeager (1935), and it measures attitude towards teachers and the teaching profession. Its author made no assumptions about correlations between the traits being studied and success in teaching, but others have used it in this connection. Results obtained by Mathews (1940), Rostker (1945), Rolfe (1945) and LaDuke (1945) suggest that the Yeager scale may have a limited usefulness in identifying teachers of different levels of efficiency. This work was all carried out in America.

Similar work in Britain, using the attitude scale *Teachers and Teaching* described in the appendix to Chapter III, supported the view that there is little, if any connection between attitude scores and practical teaching marks in the case of student teachers. (Evans, 1952a, 1953.) Reflection suggests that this is not a really surprising result. The attitude test used was concerned with many aspects of teaching as a career, and it would be quite possible for a student to have an unfavourable view of some of these, say, salary and the social position of teachers, and yet to be fully convinced of the value of the work and deeply interested in children or a subject. The attitude score of such a student might be very moderate, but he might be a much better teacher than an uncritical enthusiast. Considerations such as this help to account for the low correlations obtained.

There is some evidence, too, that the uncritical enthusiasts are likely to be found among the less intelligent students. In three training colleges, negative correlations were found between attitude scores and scores on the Moray House Adult (1) Test of Intelligence. These colleges were all in the same geographical area, and it is possible that the reason for this result may lie in the social and economic conditions there. Evidence from a fourth college, in a different area, makes it clear that the result cannot be generalised and taken as applying to all colleges. Nevertheless, interviewing panels might be wise to beware of over-enthusiastic candidates.

The test *Teachers and Teaching* is concerned with attitude to teaching as a career. Another approach is found in a test, designed to predict how well a teacher will get along with his pupils and, indirectly, how satisfied he will be with teaching as a career, which was constructed by Cook, Leeds and Callis (1951). The items used in the *Minnesota Teacher Attitude Inventory* deal with matters which are frequently studied in courses on the Theory of Education, and scores on the Inventory have been found to show a small correlation with students' marks in a written examination on this subject. (Evans, 1958.) In spite of claims made for its value in America, no correlation was found between *Inventory* scores and students' practical teaching marks. This result, taken in conjunction with evidence that students can fake high scores on the *Inventory* with great success, suggests that it is not a good instrument for use in the selection of teacher-training students in this country, though according to Arvidson (1956), it seems to be more useful with experienced teachers. A recently published paper by Herbert and Turnbull (1963) includes evidence that the *Inventory* used at intervals during training, can give indications of the probable success of students, and can also show how their attitudes develop during training. To make effective use of it in this country, re-standardisation and some rewording would be necessary, as American norms bear little relation to scores obtained by students here.

All in all, tests of attitude to teaching do not appear to be very useful in predicting teaching efficiency, but it is possible that some other attitudes may matter more. Warburton, Butcher and Forrest (1963) found that scores on tests of tendermindedness and radicalism in education were positively correlated with students' results in a teacher-training course, and that economic values as measured by the *Study of Values* gave a negative correlation. As with the *Minnesota Teacher Attitude Inventory*, significant correlations were obtained with marks in theory but not in practical teaching. This makes one suspect that the correlation does not really represent a connection between the two measures but indicates their common dependence on some other factor, probably intelligence. Answers to examination questions and responses to attitude tests are both intellectual exercises, and the intellectual ability of subjects is very likely to affect scores on both. There is no guarantee that theoretical knowledge will be translated into classroom practice, or that expressed opinions will correspond with action. For this reason, attitude scores are much more likely to correlate with marks on a theory paper than with practical teaching marks.

Attitudes, Interests and Teaching

It does not seem that knowledge of attitude scores can add much to the efficiency of procedures for selecting teachers. They may tell us something of the opinions candidates are prepared to express. They may give some indication of how the candidates are likely to do in theoretical studies, but an intelligence test would probably be a better guide here. They are unlikely to provide any information at all about the probable efficiency of the candidates as practical teachers. Altogether, the dividends obtained from using an attitude test would probably be too meagre to justify the labour of administering and scoring it.

Turning to interest, there is very little work in which a teacher's efficiency and interest in the work have been compared. In an attempt at remedying this, the test *A Teacher's Day* was prepared as a means of assessing interest in the day-to-day work which a teacher is likely to have to do. It is in the form of a narrative account of a day in the life of a teacher, and it was hoped that this would enable the different activities described to be seen in something like their real setting rather than in isolation.

The activities involved were classified under four main headings. First of all, were those concerned with the intellectual training of children, such as preparing and teaching lessons, asking and answering questions, and setting and marking written work. Then came work concerned with the social training of children. This involved all the activities designed to fit children to take their place in the society in which they live. Next, the teacher has to do work which is best described as organisation. Lastly, matters of some importance in the school are the relations between the head teacher and the staff, and between various members of the staff.

In drawing up the test *A Teacher's Day*, these four aspects of the work of a teacher were kept in mind, and twenty-three statements were underlined in which the teacher was described as doing things which might fall into one or other of these categories. A panel of twelve judges was then asked to

129

classify the underlined statements. As there was no evidence as to which aspect of a teacher's work is most important, it was decided to include the same number of statements referring to each aspect, and in the end sixteen were picked out on whose classification the judges agreed, four dealing with each of the aspects described above. The final form of the test follows.

A TEACHER'S DAY

In the following description of a teacher's day, a number of passages are underlined. Decide whether you would enjoy doing the things which they describe Miss Smith as doing. If you would enjoy it very much, write 4 on the line opposite the passage in the right hand margin.

If you would be inclined to enjoy it, write 3.

If you are doubtful about it, write 2.

If you would be inclined to dislike it, write 1.

If you would dislike it very much, write 0.

Different people will like doing different things, and there are no right or wrong answers.

When she had finished breakfast, Miss Smith set off for school. It was a fine morning, so she decided to walk. On the way she met three of her pupils and walked the rest of the way with them. They talked about the club they had been to the evening before. When she got to school, Miss Smith took off her hat and coat and went into her classroom. Soon the children began to come in. Some of them went straight to their desks, but one brought some foreign stamps and a group gathered round Miss Smith's desk and looked at them with her. When the bell rang, Miss Smith marked the register and collected the dinner money. Another bell rang and Miss Smith got her class into line and went with them to School Prayers.

Attitudes, Interests and Teaching

After Prayers, lessons began. During the first lesson Miss Smith taught her class some new work which interested them very much. They asked her a lot of questions and she did her best to answer them all. Afterwards, she gave a short test and collected the papers. At break she supervised the giving out of milk and sent the children into the playground. Then she went into the staffroom and met and talked to others members of the staff.

Miss Smith was free for the next period and she marked the test she had given earlier. At dinner time she was on duty and had dinner in the school dining room.

She had to make sure that the children behaved nicely at table.

During the first half of the afternoon, Miss Smith took a party of children to the swimming baths where they were given a lesson by the instructor. They got back in time for break, when there was a short staff meeting. One of the things discussed was the possibility of sending some of the children to a school camp. Miss Smith said she thought it a good idea and that she would be willing to go with them.

At the end of the afternoon, Miss Smith supervised the tidying up of the classroom. Just as this was finished the Head Teacher came along and chatted with Miss Smith for a few minutes. As it had begun to rain, Miss Smith decided to go home by bus, and she walked to the bus stop with two other members of the staff.

After tea, Miss Smith settled down and prepared her lessons for the next day.

Attitudes, Interests and Teaching

Occasionally, in the evening, Miss Smith used to go out to meetings arranged by the teachers in the town where she lived.

When she went shopping on Saturday mornings, Miss Smith often met and talked to the mothers of children in her class.

The sum of the votes given to the sixteen statements was used as a measure of liking for the actual work of a teacher. The separate sums of the votes for the statements in the various categories gave measures of liking for the different aspects of the work. The test-retest reliability over an interval of a month with a group of twenty-two students was found to be $+0.53$, significant at the 1% level.

Correlations with the attitude test *Teachers and Teaching* were small but significant at the 5% level in the case of eighty students in one college and twenty-eight in another. Attitude towards and interest in teaching overlap, but are not identical.

It will be realised from its content that the test *A Teacher's Day* was designed for use with women students. A similar test for use with men could be constructed if it were needed.

When the test was administered to students in training, correlations between interest scores and practical teaching marks were almost all insignificant. (Evans, 1952a.) The exceptions were those obtained for two groups of non-graduate students training to teach in secondary schools. The content of the test is probably more closely connected with work in secondary schools than with other types of teaching, but this argument does not account for the insignificant correlations obtained in the case of graduates training to teach in grammar schools. (Evans, 1957.)

With this last group, correlations between interest scores and intelligence were negative and significant, and this supports the views already expressed in connection with students' attitudes. It is not the most intelligent who are most favourably inclined to teaching, and over-enthusiastic students should be regarded with suspicion. Selection of students for training should be on the basis of other factors than interest, but, at the same time, it would be folly not to take into account the candidates' desire to teach in making decisions about them.

Although interest in the work does not appear to be a good criterion of efficiency as a teacher, it is possible that a teacher's other interests may be more important. Certainly, there is a widespread belief that it is a good thing for teachers to have plenty of interests, if only because these provide points of contact with pupils. This idea is expressed in the work of Reymert (1917), Dolch (1920), Charters and Waples (1929) and Cattell (1931).

It would be a mistake, though, to overestimate the value of a teacher's interests, as Hollis (1935) found. Pupils often appreciate other qualities more, and they like teachers to be patient, friendly and fair, with a sense of humour and willing to answer questions. These are qualities which affect the atmosphere of life in the classroom and make it a comfortable place in which to work, and it is easy to see why children may be more concerned about them than about what their teachers do out of school hours.

The weight of the evidence suggests that older pupils are more appreciative of their teachers' interests than younger ones. To small children, any adult is experienced and knowledgeable, but as their own experience and knowledge grow, children need more opportunities to share their interests and to have them stimulated. It is then that they find helpful a teacher whose own interests are wide and active, but they still value one whose classroom is a place where they feel secure and happy. A teacher who can combine these characteristics has much to offer pupils.

There is evidence that wide and varied interests contribute to the mental adjustment of teachers, but this would be true of any vocational group. Teachers are, after all, human beings first and foremost, and have the same needs as other people, though some studies seem to have overlooked this point. On the whole, the bulk of the evidence suggests that teachers do not have distinct patterns of interest. At the same time, it is possible that some types of interest mark out the better teachers. For example, Knight (1922) found that the better teachers showed a slight tendency to prefer what are usually considered to be the 'harder' subjects of the curriculum.

Most student teachers have a fairly wide range of interests, which they pursue with varying degrees of activity, but it is doubtful whether these are related to their efficiency as teachers. Evidence on this produced by Evans (1957) and Warburton, Butcher and Forrest (1963) is conflicting. Possibly the student who directs his energy into a few main channels may become a better teacher than one who fritters away his energy on many interests. It is possible, too, that some students have sufficient mental and physical energy to be successful at their work and also to pursue a number of outside interests, while others may need to conserve their energy if they are to become successful teachers.

Although the attitudes and interests of the teacher may not be amongst the primary factors conditioning efficiency, they may still exert an important effect on the pupils. On controversial questions, teachers who believe it is their duty to indoctrinate may influence pupils to conform with their views. Manske (1936) found that the attitudes of some classes were more affected in this way than those of others, irrespective of the age, intelligence or socio-economic status of the pupils. It was not a question of their regard for the teacher, either. The teacher with pronounced views and a sense of mission is definitely a person to be reckoned with, and, if he were not, he would not be much use as a teacher of anything. Teachers are employed to influence their pupils, but there is still the question of who is to decide what doctrines are to be put before children in school.

Apart from definite indoctrination, some attitudes of the teacher may produce results which are not necessarily intended. Studies by Lippitt and White (1943, 1947) and by Anderson and his colleagues (1945, 1946) made it clear that the attitudes of the teachers to the pupils had a considerable effect on classroom relations. Where the teacher was auto-cratic or dominating, the children were likely to be aggressive or over-submissive. They showed little pride in their work, and they did not co-operate well with one another. In the classroom of the democratic or socially integrative teacher, on the other hand, the children were relaxed and friendly, they worked well together, and they were interested in what they were doing. Careful observation made it clear that these differences in the children were the results of the differences in the attitudes towards them of their teachers. There is ample evidence that pupils reflect, in the classroom at least, the attitudes of their teachers.

It is probably true to say that their attitude to the teacher affects the attitudes of the pupils to their work. With younger children in particular, liking for a subject may often result from liking for a teacher or for the classroom atmosphere associated with a teacher. Older pupils are less affected by such considerations and are more likely to respond to the interest inherent in the subject, but Corey and Beery (1938) found some evidence that dislike of a teacher does sometimes carry over to the subject, though the converse is less likely to be true. Pupils, it appears, can enjoy a teacher even if the subject taught is unpopular. It is worth remembering that early conditioning by a liked or disliked teacher is hard to overcome, and many a child probably owes a lifelong dread of arithmetic or mathematics to a teacher who caused undue anxiety during primary school years. (Biggs, 1959.) Corey and Beery (1938) also found a tendency for dislike of a teacher at school to prevent students from taking his subject later at college. The teacher who has little sympathy with the pupils, and does not understand their needs, may induce a dislike of school and school work which may affect the whole of their after lives.

Teachers may be able to disguise their attitudes both from themselves and outside observers, but they are still likely to influence their pupils. Symonds (1950) suggested that the personality of a teacher can be studied best by watching the reactions of pupils. Sincerity is an important quality in a teacher, and one to which pupils respond. The teacher who is confident and secure, who is interested in children and able to accept them as they are, is likely to be successful, but the teacher who is insecure, critical of the system and of people and conditions of work, is often critical, sarcastic and authoritative towards the pupils. This kind of maladjusted teacher will tend to impose a barrier between himself and the children, and neither he nor they will be likely to be happy in the classroom.

Birkinshaw (1935) thought that happiness in the work was a good criterion of success as a teacher, and found that those teachers who enjoyed their work were interested in and liked people, and had themselves had a happy childhood and enjoyed their schooldays. This sounds rather like a description of any socially well-adjusted person, and general social maladjustment seems to be characteristic of many unhappy teachers. Both Birkinshaw (1935) and Champ (1948) found evidence in support of this view.

A dislike for being one of a large group does not, by itself, necessarily imply that a person will not be a good teacher. Evans (1952a) obtained information from a large number of students about the size of the group to which they preferred to belong for a number of social activities, and sorted out those who showed a marked preference for large groups, small groups, one companion or solitude. No indication was found that preference for a group of a particular size was linked with any particular level of teaching ability. The marks of students who disliked large groups were spread through the entire range of teaching marks.

Apart from their like or dislike of large groups, people differ considerably in their capacity for knowing others. This is the quality which is sometimes called social expansiveness. A distinction should be made between this and what may be called the capacity for being known by others, for it does not follow that people who know others well are themselves well known in return. The stars of a group may not know all their admirers, but it is very likely that the admirers will feel that they know the stars. When students were asked to mark off on a list the names of all the other students in their group whom they knew well, information was also automatically provided about the people who claimed to know them. The results showed a distinct tendency for the better known students to be somewhat better teachers than the less well known, but the number of acquaintances claimed by individual students did not bear any relation to teaching marks. It seems that it is more important for a teacher to be the kind of person that the pupils can feel they know than for him to feel he knows the pupils well. A teacher whose prevailing attitude is shy but friendly may do more for his pupils than one who is more extraverted in his approach, possibly because he is less likely to make them feel the need for defensiveness on their part.

Support for this view came from the work of Phillips (1953). Using a controlled projection test, he obtained scores for a group of training college students on a number of personality attributes, and found that three gave appreciable product-moment correlations with teaching marks. These he called sympathetic understanding of children, friendliness and good disposition, and emotional stability. The multiple correlation with teaching marks was +0·81.

In view of these results, it is pertinent to enquire what conditions the attitudes of teachers towards their pupils. Burroughs (1951) found that acceptability as a pupil at school depended largely on social and athletic qualities. Birchmore (1951) was concerned about factors which caused bad relationships between pupils and teachers, and found that the staff's pleasure in teaching individual pupils was most affected by behaviour such as laziness, disobedience, inattention and insolence which was seen as being in the nature of an attack upon the teacher. The achievement of the boys, rather than the effort they put into their work, was what the staff valued, and a similar result was obtained by Chetcuti (1961).

Birchmore also noted that there seemed to be a connection

between the occupations of the boys' fathers and the pleasure the staff got out of teaching them. The subject being taught came into the picture, too, and relations with pupils were usually less good in a second subject taught than they were in the teacher's main subject.

Allied with the attitudes of pupils and teachers towards one another is the attitude of pupils towards the idea of becoming teachers themselves. The test *Teachers and Teaching* described in Chapter III was constructed with a view to determining this. When it was administered to grammar school pupils in 1946, they were found to have, on the average, a slightly favourable attitude to teaching as a career. It might be interesting to discover whether changed economic conditions have resulted in any change in this state of affairs. Earlier studies by Austin (1931), Valentine (1934) and Tudhope (1944) suggested that the prestige of teaching increased during the years of depression in Britain because of the relative security it offered compared with some other types of work.

The only factor definitely found to correlate positively with inclination towards teaching was the pupils' attitude towards school. If they liked school, they thought favourably of teaching as a career. Their achievement at school, on the other hand, was negatively correlated with their attitude to teaching, and so was their attitude to working with their hands. Pupils whose interests were predominantly practical had a significantly less favourable attitude, on the average, towards teaching than those whose interests were predominantly academic or social.

A subsidiary enquiry produced the information that the attitudes of graduate students were less favourable than those of non-graduates, though neither group showed unfavourable attitudes. This calls to mind the recurring negative correlations between attitude to and interest in teaching and other factors such as intelligence and achievement which were mentioned earlier in this chapter.

The picture of the potential student teacher which emerges from this work is of someone who has enjoyed school but not been outstandingly good at school work, and who is not much interested in practical subjects. This is startlingly like some of the popular stereotypes of teachers. It does not follow that this is a picture of a good teacher.

A good deal of criticism is sometimes levelled at teacher-training courses and some students are dissatisfied and make sweeping statements about them, not all of which are justified. In the main, according to Phillips (1932) and Charlton, Stewart and Paffard (1960), students tend to express cautious approval of their training courses, but according to Thimme Gowda (1948) their opinions bear little relation to their success.

Pupils' liking for school has been mentioned as conditioning their attitude to teaching, and many factors influence this. Streaming as a method of organisation has come in for much discussion lately, and both Pearce (1958) and Chetcuti (1961) found that, in secondary schools, it tended to lower the morale of the duller pupils. They did, however, rate their schools more highly than brighter ones sometimes did, and friend-ships mattered more in lower streams than in higher ones. The brighter pupils, though, felt more accepted by their teachers and were more satisfied with their own progress.

Whatever the type of school or system of organisation, it is not to be expected that it will provide equal benefits for all pupils. Futcher (1960) found little evidence to support the hypothesis that life and work in a comprehensive school had a beneficial effect on the confidence of pupils and promoted more democratic social behaviour than did schools organised in other ways. The truth probably is that if a school is good enough, its pupils will benefit whatever the type of organ-isation, but it is extremely difficult for any one school to provide equal satisfactions for the wide variety of pupils it is likely to contain.

The days are long since gone, if they ever existed, when schools took little account of the needs and interests of their pupils. The great number of studies of children's interests to which reference has already been made is witness to this, and the child-centred curriculum today has a real existence. At the same time, syllabuses are often drawn up with the development of the subject rather than the pupil in mind. Goldman (1962) has demonstrated the extent to which this is done in religious education. Musgrove (1963) enquired about pupils' attitudes to history of various kinds, and found a surprising unanimity in their responses. All showed a marked preference for active methods of learning and teaching history, and social and economic history had a stronger appeal at all ages than political and constitutional, though these were not rejected. Sex differences were apparent only in attitudes to military history. No support was found for the view that local or recent history makes a strong appeal to secondary modern pupils, and the general tendency was to prefer the history of far away and long ago.

The extent to which syllabuses can or should be built around children's interests is controversial. Entwistle (1963) criticises the teaching of social studies or civics instead of geography and history on the grounds that they are not as interesting to children as adults think they are. His contention that what is happening here and now is not regarded by children with any marked enthusiasm finds support in Musgrove's work. If we are going to base the curriculum on children's interests, let us first be quite certain we know what those interests are. Entwistle goes on, though, to suggest that it is the child's best interests, not his present and ephemeral ones, which must be considered, and that these latter, concrete and trivial though they may be, should be used only as a point of departure. It is the teacher's function to provide inspiration and use his greater knowledge and experience to create interest and lead the children to search for the 'solid joys and lasting treasure' waiting to be found by those who can appreciate their value.

XII

CONCLUSION

AS WAS EXPLAINED in the Preface, this book is intended as an introduction to some of the work on attitudes and interests which has been published since about 1930. No one reading it can have any real doubt that attitudes and interests do not occur spontaneously. They are the results of the conditions under which people live and the treatment they receive from earliest childhood. In other words, they are the results of education, using the term in the widest sense.

Just as we can arrange for our children to acquire particular information and to learn particular skills, so we can arrange for them to acquire particular attitudes and interests. The techniques needed are fairly well understood, and the success achieved will depend, in both cases, on the quality of the education given and the capacities of the pupils to benefit from it.

There is fairly general agreement over the subject matter that should be taught in our schools, but there is more controversy over the attitudes and interests children should develop as they grow up. In schools of all types, children are prepared for the same public examinations and so follow the same syllabuses. Attitudes are a different matter, and many parents base their preferences for schools for their children on the attitudes which they believe those schools foster.

They are undoubtedly right in believing that the attitudes a child learns will have a real and lasting effect. It is impossible, and undesirable, to control all the influences to which children are subjected in the course of their daily lives,

Conclusion

but parents and teachers can control a great many of them and home and school are the most constant influences on children. The attitudes current in these are daily impressed on them, and so may be expected to be learnt more thoroughly than those encountered elsewhere.

Very many parents plan carefully the upbringing of their children. Schools, too, tend to have their own codes, to which they try to induce pupils to conform. Because a child has only two parents but meets at school many teachers, whose views may differ, the influence of the home is likely to be more consistent than that of the school. At school, too, children from many homes are thrown together and influence one another. In this way, a child usually escapes the dangers of too concentrated indoctrination and learns to appreciate many points of view.

The problem in education is to provide children with a stable framework and, at the same time, to leave them free to grow in their own ways. To legislate for the education of children is a great responsibility and a task which should not be approached lightly. In what ways is it good, for them and for society, that they should develop and how can they best be helped to do this?

The first question is really philosophical, and we are all philosophers enough to be able to attempt to answer it. The answers will vary, from person to person, from society to society, and from time to time. This does not mean that we can shrug our shoulders and ignore the question as being unanswerable. There is an answer for us, here and now, and unless we supply it, as a community, our children will receive only a haphazard education, here and now. If this happens, we, they and succeeding generations will suffer. We cannot escape the necessity for taking decisions because the world is changing.

The second question is one which a psychologist can help to answer, and this book is an attempt at doing so. General rules can be vague and can seem irrelevant, so particular attitudes have been considered and particular experiments

Conclusion

described. In selecting these, the author has made philosophical decisions about what attitudes and experiments are educationally important. Even psychologists are people and have their predilections.

Children grow up in society and react to its authority. How they do so affects society itself, and society's reactions, in turn, affect the views children acquire about themselves. World society is made up of many groups, and their attitudes to one another affect the well-being of all mankind. It was considerations such as these that prompted the choice of attitudes to authority and to the self and intergroup attitudes for discussion.

Rapid changes which appear to be taking place in society and in international relations make it very likely that new studies will have to be made of problems in these fields. If this proves to be the case, the basic methods described here will still be of use. New research is founded on existing knowledge, and new techniques evolve from old ones. What is important is that no result shall be considered as providing a final answer, and that educationists shall go on asking questions about their aims and methods.

Interests are important to individuals, but the interests of individuals may influence society. Society may suffer, too, if children grow up to be aimless and apathetic adults, lacking interest in what goes on around them and feeling no inclination to take part in the life of the community. This can easily happen in towns and cities where people feel anonymous. Common interests can help to bind groups together and give individuals a sense of purpose. Few things contribute more to individual happiness and well-being than a sense of belonging and the chance to pursue interesting occupations.

Interests, like attitudes, are learned. It is not enough to leave children free to do what they like and hope they will discover their own interests. They may, indeed, discover interests, but not because they are free. If parents and teachers do not guide children, they will find other guides and these may be much less desirable. A little trouble taken, when

Conclusion

children are young, to introduce them to a variety of interests is likely to pay good dividends in their later happiness and in freedom from later worry for their elders.

It is not necessary to look for highly specialised interests for children. To them, the world is new, and many occupations to which adults are accustomed are exciting to children. Parents and teachers who have an adult understanding of a child's outlook can be very stimulating companions in its everyday life.

Nothing can compare with first-hand observation and involvement with real children as a means of understanding them and their needs, but knowledge of what other people have observed, and of their interpretation of it, can add depth and meaning to personal experience. That is the justification for books about education. If this one throws even a little light on attitudes and interests as important ingredients in education for living, then its writing will have been worthwhile.

BIBLIOGRAPHY

ADAMS, R. S. (1962): 'A further approach to attitude scaling.' *Brit. J. Educ. Psychol.*, 32, 201–8.

ADLER, A. (1930): 'Individual Psychology,' in Murchison, C. (Ed.) (1930): *Psychologies of 1930*. Worcester, Mass.: Clark University Press.

ADORNO, T. W., FRENKEL-BRUNSWIK, E., LEVINSON, D. J. and SANFORD, R. N. (1950): *The Authoritarian Personality*. New York: Harper.

ALLPORT, G. W. (1935): 'Attitudes,' in Murchison, C. (Ed.) (1935): *A Handbook of Social Psychology*. London: O.U.P.

ALLPORT, G. W. (1937): *Personality*. London: Constable.

ALLPORT, G. W. and VERNON, P. E. (1931): *A Study of Values*. Boston: Houghton Mifflin.

ALLPORT, G. W., VERNON, P. E. and LINDZEY, G. (1960): *A Study of Values* (3rd Edition). Boston: Houghton Mifflin.

ANDERSON, H. H. *et al.* (1945, 1946, 1946): *Studies of Teachers' Classroom Personalities, I, II, III*. Applied Psychology Monographs of the American Psychological Association. Stanford University Press.

ANGUS, L. (1950): 'A comparative study of the methods of measuring interest in science and its relation to ability and achievement.' *Brit. J. Educ. Psychol.*, 20, 63–5.

ARSENIAN, S. (1942): 'Own estimate and objective measurement.' *J. Educ. Psychol.*, 33, 291–302.

ARVIDSON, G. L. (1956): *Some Factors Influencing the Achievement of First Year Secondary Modern School Children*. Unpublished Ph.D. Thesis, University of London Library.

AUSTIN, F. M. (1931): 'An analysis of the motives of adolescents for the choice of the teaching profession.' *Brit. J. Educ. Psychol.*, 1, 87–103.

BARAHENI, M. N. (1962): 'An enquiry into attitudinal concomitants of success and failure at school.' *Educ. Res.*, 5, 63–8.

Bibliography

BASS, B. M. (1963): 'Authoritarianism or acquiescence?', in Mednick, M. T. and Mednick, S. A. (1963): *Research in Personality*. New York: Holt, Rinehart and Winston.

BATH, J. A. and LEWIS, E. C. (1962): 'Attitudes of young female adults toward some areas of parent-adolescent conflict.' *J. Genet. Psychol.*, 100, 241–53.

BECKER, M. G. and LOOMIS, C. P. (1948): 'Measuring rural urban and farm and non-farm cleavages in a rural consolidated school.' *Sociometry*, 11, 246–61.

BENNETT, E. B. (1955): 'Discussion, decision, commitment and consensus in "group decision".' *Human Relations*, 8, 251–73.

BERDIE, R. F. (1943): 'Factors associated with vocational interests.' *J. Educ. Psychol.*, 34, 257–77.

BERDIE, R. F. (1944): 'Factors related to vocational interests.' *Psychol. Bull.*, 41, 137–57.

BIGGS, J. B. (1959): 'The teaching of mathematics: II. Attitudes to arithmetic-number anxiety.' *Educ. Res.*, 1, 6–21.

BIRCHMORE, B. (1951): *A Study of the Relationships between Pupils and Teachers in Certain Classes in a Secondary Grammar School*. Unpublished M.A. Thesis, University of London Library.

BIRKINSHAW, M. (1935): *The Successful Teacher*. London: Hogarth Press.

BOGARDUS, E. S. (1947): 'The measurement of social distance,' in Newcomb, T. M. and Hartley, E. L. (1947): *Readings in Social Psychology*. New York: Henry Holt.

BOYNTON, P. L. (1940): 'The relationship of hobbies to personality characteristics of school children.' *J. Exp. Educ.*, 8, 363–7.

BRIDGES, J. W. and DOLLINGER, V. M. (1920): 'The correlation between interests and abilities in college courses.' *Psychol. Rev.*, 27, 308–14.

BROWN, L. B. (1962): 'A study of religious belief.' *Brit. J. Psychol.*, 53, 259–72.

BROWN, L. M. (1959): *An Enquiry into Attitudes and Understandings involved in the Study of History, with Experiments in their Measurement and Modification in the Secondary School*. Unpublished Ph.D. Thesis, University of London Library.

BROWNFAIN, J. J. (1952): 'Stability of the self-concept as a dimension of personality.' *J. Abnorm. and Soc. Psychol.*, 47, 597–606.

BULL, B. M. (1954): *The Place and Nature of International Education in the Secondary Schools of England and Wales. A Study of the Attempts to Educate for International Understanding between 1919 and 1939.* Unpublished M.A. Thesis, University of Wales Library (Cardiff).

BURROUGHS, G. (1951): *Selection of Students for Training as Teachers.* Unpublished Ph.D. Thesis, University of Birmingham Library.

BURT, C. (1947): 'Symposium on the selection of pupils for different types of secondary schools: I. A general survey.' *Brit. J. Educ. Psychol.*, 17, 57–71.

CAMPBELL, D. T. (1950): 'The indirect assessment of social attitudes.' *Psychol. Bull.*, 47, 15–38.

CARRIGAN, P. M. (1960): 'Extraversion-introversion as a dimension of personality.' *Psychol. Bull.*, 57, 329–60.

CARSLEY, J. D. (1957): 'The interests of children (aged 10–11) in books.' *Brit. J. Educ. Psychol.*, 27, 13–23.

CARTER, H. D. (1932): 'Twin similarities in occupational interests.' *J. Educ. Psychol.*, 23, 641–55.

CARTER, H. D. (1940): 'The development of vocational attitudes.' *J. Consult. Psychol.*, 4, 185–91.

CARTER, H. D., PYLES, M. K. and BRETNALL, E. P. (1935): 'A comparative study of factors in vocational scores of high school boys.' *J. Educ. Psychol.*, 26, 81–98.

CATTELL, R. B. (1931): 'The assessment of teaching ability.' *Brit. J. Educ. Psychol.*, 1, 48–72.

CATTELL, R. B., MAXWELL, E. F., LIGHT, B. H. and UNGER, M. P. (1949): 'The objective measurement of attitudes.' *Brit. J. Educ. Psychol.*, 40, 81–90.

CHAMP, J. M. (1948): *A Study of the Attitude of Women Students, Teachers and Former Teachers towards Teaching as a Career.* Unpublished M.A. Thesis, University of London Library.

CHARLTON, K., STEWART, W. A. C. and PAFFARD, M. K. (1960): 'Students' attitudes to courses in Education.' *Brit. J. Educ. Studies*, 8, 148–64.

CHARTERS, W. W. and WAPLES, D. (1929): *The Commonwealth Teacher-Training Study.* Chicago: Univ. of Chicago Press.

CHETCUTI, F. (1961): 'A study of the morale of A stream and

C stream pupils in secondary schools with special references to any differences in the attitude and behaviour of their teachers.' *Educ. Rev.*, 14, 49–53.

CHISNALL, B. (1942): 'The interests and personality traits of delinquent boys.' *Brit. J. Educ. Psychol.*, 12, 76.

COOK, W. W., LEEDS, C. H. and CALLIS, R. (1951): Minnesota Teacher Attitude Inventory. New York: Psychological Corporation.

COREY, S. M. (1936): 'Attitude differences between college classes: A summary and criticism.' *J. Educ. Psychol.*, 27, 321–30.

COREY, S. M. (1937a): 'Signed *versus* unsigned attitude questionnaires.' *J. Educ. Psychol.*, 28, 144–8.

COREY, S. M. (1937b): 'Professed attitudes and actual behavior.' *J. Educ. Psychol.*, 28, 271–80.

COREY, S. M. and BEERY, G. S. (1938): 'The effect of teacher popularity upon attitude toward school subjects.' *J. Educ. Psychol.*, 29, 665–70.

CRISWELL, J. H. (1942): 'The saturation point as a sociometric concept.' *Sociometry*, 5, 146–50.

CURR, W., HALLWORTH, H. J. and WILKINSON, A. M. (1962): 'How secondary modern school children spend their time.' *Educ. Rev.*, 15, 3–11.

DARLEY, J. G. (1938): 'Preliminary study of the relationships between attitudes, adjustment and vocational interest tests.' *J. Educ. Psychol.*, 29, 467–73.

DAVIES, D. L. (1957): *A Comparative Study of some of the Intellectual, Social and Emotional Characteristics of Bilingual and Monoglot Students at a Welsh University College*. Unpublished M.A. Thesis, University of Wales Library (Cardiff).

DAVIES, J. A. (1959): *A Study of the Interests and Attitudes of Pupils at a Secondary Modern School*. Unpublished M.A. Thesis, University of Wales Library (Aberystwyth).

DIGMAN, J. M. (1962): 'The dimensionality of social attitudes.' *J. Soc. Psychol.*, 57, 433–44.

DOLCH, E. W. (1920): 'Pupils' judgments of their teachers.' *Ped. Sem.*, 27, 195–9.

DROBA, D. D. (1932): 'Methods for measuring attitudes.' *Psychol. Bull.*, 29, 309–23.

Bibliography

DUFFY, E. (1940): 'A critical review of investigations employing the Allport-Vernon Study of Values and other tests of evaluative attitudes.' *Psychol. Bull.*, 37, 597–612.

DUFFY, E. and CRISSY, W. J. E. (1940): 'Evaluative attitudes as related to vocational interests and academic achievement.' *J. Abnorm. and Soc. Psychol.*, 35, 226–45.

DUKES, W. F. (1955): Psychological studies of values.' *Psychol. Bull.*, 52, 24–50.

EDWARDS, A. L. (1957): *Techniques of Attitude Scale Construction.* New York: Appleton-Century-Crofts.

EGNER, R. E. and OBELSKY, A. J. (1957): 'Effect of stereotyped attitudes on learning.' *J. Educ. Psychol.*, 48, 207–12.

EMMETT, R. G. (1959): *A Psychological Study of the Self-Concept amongst a Group of Pupils in a Secondary Modern School.* Unpublished M.A. Thesis, University of London Library.

ENGLISH, H. B. and ENGLISH, A. V. (1958): *A Comprehensive Dictionary of Psychological and Psychoanalytical Terms.* London: Longmans Green.

ENTWISTLE, H. (1963): 'Education by slogan.' *Studies in Education (University of Hull)*, 3, 403–12.

EVANS, E. E. (1962): *Verse Writing by Children. An Investigation of Some of its Effects on their Writing of Prose and their Attitude to Poetry.* Unpublished M.A. Thesis, University of Wales Library (Cardiff).

EVANS, K. M. (1946): *A Study of Attitude towards Teaching as a Career.* Unpublished M.A. Thesis, University of London Library.

EVANS, K. M. (1952a): *A Study of Teaching Ability at the Training College Stage in relation to the Personality and Attitudes of the Student.* Unpublished Ph.D. Thesis, University of London Library.

EVANS, K. M. (1952b): 'A study of attitude towards teaching as a career.' *Brit. J. Educ. Psychol.*, 22, 63–70.

EVANS, K. M. (1953): 'A further study of attitude towards teaching as a career.' *Brit. J. Educ. Psychol.*, 23, 58–63.

EVANS, K. M. (1957): 'Is the concept of "interest" of significance to success in a teacher training course?' *Educ. Rev.*, 9, 205–11.

EVANS, K. M. (1958): 'An examination of the Minnesota Teacher Attitude Inventory.' *Brit. J. Educ. Psychol.*, 28, 253–7.

Bibliography

EVANS, K. M. (1960): *Club Members Today*. London: National Association of Mixed Clubs and Girls' Clubs.

EYSENCK, H. J. (1951a): 'Primary social attitudes and the "Social Insight" test.' *Brit. J. Psychol.*, 42, 114–22.

EYSENCK, H. J. (1951b): 'Primary social attitudes as related to social class and political party.' *Brit. J. Sociol.*, 2, 198–209.

EYSENCK, H. J. (1953a): 'Primary social attitudes. II. A comparison of attitude patterns in England, Germany and Sweden.' *J. Abnorm. and Soc. Psychol.*, 48, 563–8.

EYSENCK, H. J. (1953b and 1960): *The Structure of Human Personality*. London: Methuen.

EYSENCK, H. J. (1954): *Psychology of Politics*. London: Routledge and Kegan Paul.

FAUNCE, D. and BEEGLE, J. A. (1948): 'Cleavages in a relatively homogeneous group of rural youth.' *Sociometry*, 11, 207–16.

FEAKES, B. A. (1953): *A Study in the Changing of Attitudes towards Foreign Peoples by Educational Means*. Unpublished M.A. Thesis, University of London Library.

FERGUSON, L. W. (1939a): 'Primary social attitudes.' *J. Psychol.*, 8, 217–23.

FERGUSON, L. W. (1939b): 'The requirements of an adequate attitude scale.' *Psychol. Bull.*, 37, 665–73.

FERGUSON, L. W. (1940): 'The measurement of primary social attitudes.' *J. Psychol.*, 10, 199–205.

FERGUSON, L. W., HUMPHREYS, L. G. and STRONG, F. W. (1941): 'A factorial analysis of interests and values.' *J. Educ. Psychol.*, 32, 197–204.

FITZPATRICK, T. F. and WISEMAN, S. (1954): 'An interest test for use in selection for technical education.' *Brit. J. Educ. Psychol.*, 24, 99–105.

FLEMING, C. M. (Ed.) (1951): *Studies in the Social Psychology of Adolescence*. London: Routledge and Kegan Paul.

FLEMING, C. M. (1959): *Cotswold Personality Assessment (P.A. 1)* Glasgow: Robert Gibson.

FLEMING, C. M., DIGARIA, D. F. and NEWTH, H. G. R. (1960): 'Preferences and values among adolescent boys and girls.' *Educ. Res.*, 3, 221–4.

FLETCHER, R. (1962): *Britain in the Sixties. The Family and Marriage*. London: Penguin.

FLOOD, W. E. and CROSSLAND, R. W. (1947): 'The origins of

interest and motives for the study of natural sciences and psychology among students in voluntary courses.' *Brit. J. Educ. Psychol.*, 17, 105–17.

FORRESTER, J. F. (1951): 'The attitudes of adolescents towards their own development,' in Fleming, C. M. (Ed.) (1951), *Studies in the Social Psychology of Adolescence*. London: Routledge and Kegan Paul.

FRENKEL-BRUNSWIK, E. (1948): 'A study of prejudice in children.' *Hum. Rel.*, 1, 295–306.

FREUD, S. (1933): *New Introductory Lectures on Psycho-Analysis*. London: Hogarth Press and The Institute of Psycho-Analysis.

FREUD, S. (1949): *An Outline of Psycho-Analysis*. London: Hogarth Press and The Institute of Psycho-Analysis.

FRYER, D. (1923): 'Intelligence and interest in vocational adjustment.' *Ped. Sem.*, 30, 127–51.

FRYER, D. (1931): *The Measurement of Interests*. New York: Henry Holt.

FUTCHER, W. G. A. (1960): *A Comparative Study of Attitudes and Personality Traits of Children in Certain Comprehensive, Grammar and Modern Schools in London*. Unpublished M.A. Thesis, University of London Library.

GEORGE, E. I. (1954): *An Experimental Study of the Relations between Personal Values, Social Attitudes and Personality Traits*. Unpublished Ph.D. Thesis, University of London Library.

GLASSEY, W. (1945): 'The attitude of grammar school pupils and their parents to education, religion and sport.' *Brit. J. Educ. Psychol.*, 15, 101–4.

GOLDMAN, R. J. (1962): *Some Aspects of the Development of Religious Thinking in Childhood and Adolescence*. Dept. of Education, The University, Reading.

GREEN, G. H. (1932): 'Have children a national bias?' *Discovery*, 13, 44–6.

GUILFORD, J. P. (1959): *Personality*. New York: McGraw-Hill.

GUTTMAN, L. (1941): 'The quantification of a class of attributes: A theory and method of scale construction,' in Horst, P. (1941): *The Prediction of Personal Adjustment*. New York: Social Science Research Council.

Bibliography

GUTTMAN, L. (1947): 'The Cornell technique for scale and intensity analysis.' *Educ. and Psychol. Meas.*, 7, 247–79.

GUTTMAN, L. (1950): 'The basis for scalogram analysis,' in Stouffer, S. A. (1950): *Measurement and Prediction.* Princeton: Princeton University Press.

HAMMOND, W. H. (1945): 'An analysis of Youth Centre interests.' *Brit. J. Educ. Psychol.*, 15, 122–6.

HARRIS, H. (1949): The Group Approach to Leadership Testing. London: Routledge and Kegan Paul.

HARTMAN, R. and DASHIELL, J. F. (1919): 'An experiment to determine the relation of interests to abilities.' *Psych. Bull.*, 16, 259–62.

HERBERT, N. and TURNBULL, G. H. (1963): 'Personality factors and effective progress in teaching.' *Educ. Rev.*, 16, 24–31.

H.M.S.O. (1963): *Half Our Future* (Newsom Report). London: H.M.S.O.

HINCKLEY, E. D. (1932): 'The influence of individual opinion on the construction of an attitude scale.' *J. Soc. Psychol.*, 3, 283–96.

HOLLIS, A. W. (1935): *The Personal Relationship in Teaching.* Unpublished M.A. Thesis, University of Birmingham Library.

HORNEY, K. (1946): *Our Inner Conflicts.* London: Kegan Paul, Trench, Trubner.

HOROWITZ, E. L. (1947): 'Development of attitude toward Negroes,' in Newcomb, T. M. and Hartley, E. L. (Ed.) (1947): *Readings in Social Psychology.* New York: Henry Holt.

HOVLAND, C. I. (1951): 'Changes in attitude through communication.' *J. Abnorm. and Soc. Psychol.*, 46, 424–37.

HUGHES, E. W. (1955): 'Children's choices in individual activities in the junior school.' *Brit. J. Educ. Psychol.*, 25, 36–50.

HYDE, K. E. (1963): 'Religious concepts and religious attitudes.' *Educ. Rev.*, 15, 132–41 and 217–27.

JACKSON, L. (1950): 'Emotional attitude towards the family of normal, neurotic and delinquent children.' *Brit. J. Psychol.*, 41, 35–51 and 173–85.

JAHODA, G. (1963): 'The development of children's ideas about country and nationality. I. The conceptual framework. II.

Bibliography

National symbols and themes.' *Brit. J. Educ. Psychol.*, 33, 47–60 and 143–53.

JAMES, W. (1890): *Principles of Psychology*. London: Macmillan.

JAMES, W. (1925): *Pragmatism*. New York: Longmans.

JAMES, H. E. O. and TENEN, C. (1950): 'How adolescents think of peoples.' *Brit. J. Psychol. (Gen. Section)*, 41, 145–72.

JAMES, H. E. O. and TENEN, C. (1953): *The Teacher Was Black*. London: Heinemann.

JAYATILAKA, I. W. DE S. (1951): *A Study of a Change of Attitude of Post-graduate Students in the Institute of Education, 1949–50*. Unpublished M.A. Thesis, University of London Library.

JENKINS, A. G. (1962): *The Construction of Tests for a Mixed Language Population*. Unpublished M.A. Thesis, University of Wales Library (Cardiff).

JENKINSON, A. J. (1940): *What Do Boys and Girls Read?* London: Methuen.

JERSILD, A. T. (1952): *In Search of Self*. New York: Teachers College, Columbia University.

JOHNSON, D. M. (1945): 'A systematic treatment of judgment.' *Psychol. Bull.*, 42, 193–224.

JOHNSON, D. G. (1953): 'Effect of vocational counselling on self-knowledge.' *Educ. and Psychol. Meas.*, 13, 330–8.

JONES, J. A. (1962): *An Investigation into the Responses of Boys and Girls respectively to Scripture as a School Subject in Certain Co-educational Grammar Schools in Industrial South Wales*. Unpublished M.A. Thesis, University of Wales Library (Swansea).

JONES, V. (1938): 'Attitudes of college students and the changes in such attitudes during four years in college.' *J. Educ. Psychol.*, 29, 14–25 and 114–34.

JONES, W. R. (1949): 'Attitude towards Welsh as a second language: A preliminary investigation.' *Brit. J. Educ. Psychol.*, 19, 44–52.

JONES, W. R. (1950): 'Attitude towards Welsh as a second language.' *Brit. J. Educ. Psychol.*, 20, 117–32.

JORDAN, D. (1937): *An Analysis of the Attitude of Children towards certain School Subjects, and the Measure of Correlation between Attitude and Attainment*. Unpublished M.A. Thesis, University of London Library.

Bibliography

JUNG, C. G. (1923): *Psychological Types*. London: Kegan Paul, Trench, Trubner.

KEEHN, J. D. (1955): 'An examination of the two-factor theory of social attitudes in a Near Eastern culture.' *J. Soc. Psychol.*, 42, 13–20.

KELMAN, H. C. (1953): 'Attitude change as a function of response restriction.' *Hum. Rel.*, 6, 185–214.

KELMAN, H. C. (1962): 'The induction of action and attitude change,' in Coopersmith, S. (Ed.) *Proceedings of the XIV International Congress of Applied Psychology. III. Personality Research*. Copenhagen: Munksgaard.

KHAN, S. (1954): *An Experiment in Changing Attitudes towards Other Peoples*. Unpublished M.A. Thesis, University of London Library.

KING, B. T. and JANIS, I. L. (1956). 'Comparison of the effectiveness of improvised *versus* non-improvised role playing in producing opinion changes.' *Hum. Rel.*, 9, 177–86.

KNIGHT, F. B. (1922): *Qualities Related to Success in Teaching*. New York: Teachers College, Columbia University.

KROUT, M. H. and STAGNER, R. (1939): 'Personality development in radicals.' *Sociometry*, 2, 31–46.

KUDER, G. F. (1956): *Kuder Preference Record (6th Edn.)*. Illinois: Science Research Associates.

KULP, D. H. and DAVIDSON, H. H. (1933): 'Sibling resemblance in social attitudes.' *J. Educ. Sociol.*, 7, 133–40.

LADUKE, C. V. (1945): 'The evaluation of teaching ability.' *J. Exp. Educ.*, 14, 75–100.

LAHIRY, M. (1960): *A Study of the Attitudes of Adolescent Girls to their own Physical, Intellectual, Emotional and Social Development*. Unpublished M.A. Thesis, University of London Library.

LAMBERT, C. M. (1944): *A Study of Interest in School Subjects among Secondary School Pupils*. Unpublished M.A. Thesis, University of London Library.

LAMBERT, C. M. (1949): 'Symposium on selection of pupils for different types of secondary schools. VII. A survey of ability and interest at the stage of transfer.' *Brit. J. Educ. Psychol.*, 19, 67–81.

LAMBERT, C. M. and PEEL, E. A.: *General Information Test*.

Bibliography

LENTZ, T. F. (1938): 'Generality and specificity of conservatism-radicalism.' *J. Educ. Psychol.*, 29, 540–6.

LEWIN, K. (1947a): 'Group decision and social change,' in Newcomb, T. M. and Hartley, E. L. (Ed.) (1947): *Readings in Social Psychology*. New York: Henry Holt.

LEWIN, K. (1947b): 'Frontiers in group dynamics.' *Hum. Rel.*, 1, 5–41, and 143–53.

LIKERT, R. (1932): 'A technique for the measurement of attitudes.' *Archives of Psychology*, 22, 5–55.

LIKERT, R., ROSLOW, S., MURPHY, G. (1934): 'A simple and reliable method of scoring the Thurstone attitude scales.' *J. Soc. Psychol.*, 5, 228–38.

LINTON, R. (1947): *The Cultural Background of Personality*. London: Kegan Paul, Trench, Trubner.

LIPPITT, R. and WHITE, R. K. (1943): 'The "social climate" of children's groups,' in Barker, R. G., Kounin, J. S. and Wright, H. F. (1943): *Child Behaviour and Development*. New York: McGraw-Hill.

LIPPITT, R. and WHITE, R. K. (1947): 'An experimental study of leadership and group life,' in Newcomb, T. M. and Hartley, E. L. (Ed.) (1947): *Readings in Social Psychology*. New York: Henry Holt.

LOVELL, K. and WHITE, G. E. (1958): 'Some influences affecting choice of subjects in school and training college.' *Brit. J. Educ. Psychol.*, 28, 15–24.

LURIE, W. A. (1937): 'A study of Spranger's value-types by the method of factor analysis.' *J. Soc. Psychol.*, 8, 17–37.

MACFARLANE, J. C. (1950): *A Study of the Choices of Careers in a Group of Adolescents*. Unpublished M.A. Thesis, University of London Library.

MCNEMAR, Q. (1946): 'Opinion-attitude methodology.' *Psychol. Bull.*, 43, 289–374.

MANSKE, A. J. (1936): *The Reflection of Teachers' Attitudes in the Attitudes of their Pupils*. New York: Teachers College, Columbia University.

MATHEWS, L. H. (1940): 'An item analysis of measures of teaching ability.' *J. Educ. Res.*, 33, 576–80.

MEAD, G. M. (1934): *Mind, Self and Society*. Chicago: University of Chicago Press.

Bibliography

MEDNICK, M. T. and MEDNICK, S. A. (1963): *Research in Personality*. New York: Holt, Rinehart and Winston.

MELVIN, D. (1955): *An Experimental and Statistical Study of the Primary Social Attitudes*. Unpublished Ph.D. Thesis, University of London Library.

MEYER, G. R. and PENFOLD, D. M. E. (1961): 'Symposium: Studies of Children's Scientific Concepts: III. Factors associated with interest in science.' *Brit. J. Educ. Psychol.*, 31, 33–7.

MILLER, K. M. and BIGGS, J. B. (1958): 'Attitude change through undirected group discussion.' *J. Educ. Psychol.*, 49, 224–8.

MISTRY, Z. D. (1960): *A Study of the Self-picture as held by Selected Groups of Adolescent Girls prior to and after School-leaving Age*. Unpublished M.A. Thesis, University of London Library.

MORENO, J. L. (1953): *Who Shall Survive? Foundations of Sociometry, Group Psychotherapy and Sociodrama*. Beacon, New York: Beacon House.

MURCHISON, C. (1935): *A Handbook of Social Psychology*. London: O.U.P.

MURPHY, G., MURPHY, L. B. and NEWCOMB, T. M. (1937): *Experimental Social Psychology*. New York: Harper.

MUSGROVE, F. (1963): 'Five scales of attitude to history.' *Studies in Education (University of Hull)*, 3, 423–39.

MYERS, G. C. (1921): 'Control of conduct by suggestion: An experiment in Americanisation.' *J. Appl. Psychol.*, 5, 26–31.

NELSON, E. (1939): 'Attitudes: Their nature and development.' *J. General Psychol.*, 21, 367–99, 401–16, 417–36.

NEWCOMB, T. M. (1943): *Personality and Social Change*. New York: Dryden Press.

NEWCOMB, T. M. (1947): 'Some patterned consequences of membership of a college community,' in Newcomb, T. M. and Hartley, E. L. (Ed.) (1947): *Readings in Social Psychology*. New York: Henry Holt.

NEWCOMB, T. M. and HARTLEY, E. L. (Ed.) (1947): *Readings in Social Psychology*. New York: Henry Holt.

NEWCOMB, T. M. and SVEHLA, G.: 'Intra-family relationships in attitude.' *Sociometry*, 1, 180–205.

PACE, C. R. (1950): 'Opinion and action: A study in validity of attitude measurement.' *Educ. and Psychol. Meas.*, 10, 411–9.

PEARCE, R. A. (1958): 'Streaming and a sociometric study.' *Educ. Rev.*, 10, 248–51.

PEEL, E. A. (1948): 'Assessment of interest in practical topics.' *Brit. J. Educ. Psychol.*, 18, 41–7.

PEEL, E. A. (1949): 'Symposium on the selection of pupils for different types of secondary schools. VI. Evidence of a practical factor at the age of eleven.' *Brit. J. Educ. Psychol.*, 19, 1–15.

PEEL, E. A. (1959): 'Experimental examination of some of Piaget's schemata concerning children's perception and thinking, and a discussion of their educational significance.' *Brit. J. Educ. Psychol.*, 29, 89–103.

PETERSON, R. C. and THURSTONE, L. L. (1932): 'Effect of a motion picture film on children's attitudes towards Germans.' *J. Educ. Psychol.*, 23, 241–6.

PHILLIPS, A. S. (1953): *An Examination of Methods of Selection of Training College Students.* Unpublished M.A. Thesis, University of London Library.

PHILLIPS, M. (1932): 'Professional courses in the training of teachers.' *Brit. J. Educ. Psychol.*, 1, 225–45 and 2, 1–24.

PIAGET, J. (1928): *Judgment and Reasoning in the Child.* London: Routledge and Kegan Paul.

PINTNER, R. and FORLANO, G. (1937): 'The influence of attitude upon scaling of attitude items.' *J. Soc. Psychol.*, 8, 39–45.

PRITCHARD, R. A. (1935): 'The relative popularity of secondary school subjects at various ages.' *Brit. J. Educ. Psychol.*, 5, 157–79 and 229–41.

RADKE, M. J. (1946): *The Relation of Parental Authority to Children's Behaviour and Attitudes.* Minneapolis: University of Minnesota Press.

RADKE, M., SUTHERLAND, J. and ROSENBERG, P. (1950): 'Racial attitudes of children.' *Sociometry*, 13, 154–71.

RALLISON, R. (1939): 'The scientific interests of senior school children.' *Brit. J. Educ. Psychol.*, 9, 117–30.

REMMERS, H. H. (1954): *Introduction to Opinion and Attitude Measurement.* New York: Harper.

REYMERT, M. L. (1917): 'The psychology of the teacher: An introductory study.' *Ped. Sem.*, 24, 521–8.

Bibliography

RIVLIN, L. G. (1959): 'Creativity and the self-attitudes and sociability of High School students.' *J. Educ. Psychol.*, 50, 147–52.

ROGERS, C. R. (1959): 'A theory of therapy, personality, and inter-personal relationships, as developed in the client-centered framework,' in Koch, S. (Ed.) (1959): *Psychology: A Study of a Science. 3. Formulations of the Person in the Social Context*. New York: McGraw Hill.

ROGERS, C. R. (1961): *On Becoming a Person*. London: Constable.

ROLFE, J. F. (1945): 'The measurement of teaching ability.' *J. Exp. Educ.*, 14, 52–74.

ROSTKER, L. E. (1945): 'The measurement of teaching ability.' *J. Exp. Educ.*, 14, 6–51.

RUNDQUIST, E. A. (1940): 'Form of statement in personality measurement.' *J. Educ. Psychol.*, 135–47.

SCOTT, O. and BRINKLEY, S. G. (1960): 'Attitude changes of student teachers and validity of the Minnesota Teacher Attitude Inventory.' *J. Educ. Res.*, 51, 76–81.

SHAKESPEARE, J. J. (1936): 'An enquiry into the relative popularity of school subjects in elementary schools.' *Brit. J. Educ. Psychol.*, 6, 147–64.

SHEPPARD, D. (1963): 'Characteristics associated with Christian names.' *Brit. J. Psychol.*, 54, 167–74.

SHOBEN, E. J. (1949): 'The assessment of parental attitudes to child adjustment.' *Genet. Psychol. Monogr.*, 39, 101–48.

SMITH, E. B. (1958): *An Investigation into some of the Factors Influencing the Mathematical Attainment of Third Year Grammar School Boys, with particular reference to Attitude*. Unpublished M.Sc. Thesis, University of Wales Library (Cardiff).

SOWER, C. (1948): 'Social stratification in suburban communities.' *Sociometry*, 11, 235–43.

SPENCER, D. (1938): 'The frankness of subjects on personality measures.' *J. Educ. Psychol.*, 29, 26–35.

SPRANGER, E. (1928): *Types of Men*. Halle: Niemeyer.

STACEY, M. W. (1948): *An Enquiry into the Stability of Attitudes and Interests of a Group of Adolescent Girls*. Unpublished M.A. Thesis, University of London Library.

STAGNER, R. and DROUGHT, N. (1935): 'Measuring children's attitudes toward their parents.' *J. Educ. Psychol.*, 26, 169–76.

Bibliography

STAINES, J. W. (1958): 'Symposium: The development of children's values. III. The self-picture as a factor in the classroom.' *Brit. J. Educ. Psychol.*, 28, 97-111.

STEPHEN, J. L. (1938): *Occupational Interests in relation to Intelligence*. Unpublished M.A. Thesis, University of London Library.

STEPHENSON, W. (1936a): 'The inverted factor technique.' *Brit. J. Psychol.*, 26, 344-61.

STEPHENSON, W. (1936b): 'A new application of correlation to averages.' *Brit. J. Educ. Psychol.*, 6, 43-57.

STEPHENSON, W. (1936c): 'Introduction to inverted factor analysis with some applications to studies in orexis.' *J. Educ. Psychol.*, 27, 353-67.

STEWART, M. (1950): 'The leisure activities of grammar school children. *Brit. J. Educ. Psychol.*, 20, 11-34.

STOUFFER, S. A. *et al.* (1950): *Measurement and Prediction*. Princeton: Princeton University Press.

STRANG, R. (1957): *The Adolescent Views Himself*. New York: McGraw Hill.

STRONG, E. K. (1943): *Vocational Interests of Men and Women*. California: Stanford University Press.

STRONG, E. K. (1959): *Vocational Interest Blanks for Men and Women*. California: Consulting Psychologists Press.

SUPER, D. E. (1949): *Appraising Vocational Fitness by Means of Psychological Tests*. New York: Harper.

SYMONDS, P. M. (1950): 'Reflections on observations of teachers.' *J. Educ. Res.*, 43, 688-96.

THIMME GOWDA, T. V. (1948): *A Study of the Attitudes of Teachers in England towards their Course of Training*. Unpublished M.A. Thesis, University of London Library.

THORNDIKE, E. L. (1921): 'The correlation between interests and abilities in college courses.' *Psychol. Rev.*, 28, 374-6.

THOULESS, R. H. (1935): 'The tendency to certainty in religious belief.' *Brit. J. Psychol.*, 26, 16-31.

THURSTONE, L. L. (1927): 'The method of paired comparisons for social values.' *J. Abnorm. and Soc. Psychol.*, 21, 384-400.

THURSTONE, L. L. (1928): 'An experimental study of nationality preferences.' *J. Genet. Psychol.*, 1, 405-25.

THURSTONE, L. L. (1929): 'The theory of attitude measurement.' *Psychol. Rev.*, 36, 221-41.

Bibliography

THURSTONE, L. L. (1931): 'A multiple factor study of vocational interests.' *J. Personnel*, 10, 198–205.

THURSTONE, L. L. (1934): 'The vectors of mind.' *Psychol. Rev.*, 41, 1–32.

THURSTONE, L. L. (1959): *The Measurement of Values*. Chicago: University of Chicago Press.

THURSTONE, L. L. and CHAVE, E. J. (1929): *The Measurement of Attitude*. Chicago: University of Chicago Press.

TITUS, H. E. and HOLLANDER, E. P. (1963): 'The California F scale in psychological research: 1950–55,' in Mednick, M. T. and Mednick, S. A. (1963): *Research in Personality*. New York: Holt, Rinehart and Winston.

TORRANCE, E. P. (1954): 'Some practical uses of a knowledge of self-concepts in counselling and guidance.' *Educ. and Psychol. Meas.*, 14, 120–7.

TUDHOPE, W. B. (1944): 'Motives for the choice of the teaching profession by training college students.' *Brit. J. Educ. Psychol.*, 14, 129–41.

VALENTINE, C. W. (1934): 'An enquiry as to the choice of the teaching profession by university students.' *Brit. J. Educ. Psychol.*, 4, 237–59.

VENESS, T. (1962): *School Leavers*. London: Methuen.

VERNON, M. D. (1937 and 1938): 'The drives which determine the choice of a career.' *Brit. J. Educ. Psychol.*, 7, 302–16 and 8, 1–15.

VERNON, P. E. (1938): *The Assessment of Psychological Qualities by Verbal Methods*. London: H.M.S.O.

VERNON, P. E. (1949): 'Classifying high-grade occupational interests.' *J. Abnorm. and Soc. Psychol.*, 44, 84–96.

VERNON, P. E. (1953): *Personality Tests and Assessments*. London: Methuen.

VERNON, P. E. and ALLPORT, G. W. (1931): 'A test for personal values.' *J. Abnorm. and Soc. Psychol.*, 26, 231–48.

VINACKE, W. E., EINDHOVEN, J. and ENGLE, J. (1949): 'Religious attitudes of students at the University of Hawaii.' *J. Psychol.*, 28, 161–79.

WAKATAMA, M. A. (1957): *An Experimental Study of the Teaching of the Geography of Africa, with special reference to its*

Bibliography

Effects upon the Attitudes of English Children towards Africans. Unpublished M.A. Thesis, University of London Library.

WARBURTON, F. W., BUTCHER, H. J. and FORREST, G. M. (1963): 'Predicting student performance in a University Department of Education.' *Brit. J. Educ. Psychol.*, 33, 68–79.

WHITEHEAD, F. (1956): 'The attitude of grammar school pupils towards some novels commonly read in school.' *Brit. J. Educ. Psychol.*, 26, 104–11.

WIEGERSMA, S. and BARR, F. (1959): 'Educational guidance. II: Interest testing in educational and vocational guidance. *Educ. Res.*, 39–64.

WILLIAMS, A. R. (1951): 'The magazine reading of secondary school children.' *Brit. J. Educ. Psychol.*, 21, 186–98.

WILLIAMS, H. V. (1962): *An Investigation into the Vocational Opportunities and Choices of a Group of Children (Boys and Girls) attending a New Secondary School serving both Industrial and Rural Communities.* Unpublished M.A. Thesis, University of Wales Library (Cardiff).

WISEMAN, S. (1955): 'The use of an interest test in 11 plus selection.' *Brit. J. Educ. Psychol.*, 25, 92–8.

WISEMAN, S. and FITZPATRICK, T. F. (1955): *Devon Interest Test.* London: Oliver and Boyd.

WITMER, H. L. (1937): 'The influence of parental attitudes on the social adjustment of the individual.' *American Sociol. Rev.*, 2, 756–63.

WRIGHT, D. S. (1962): 'A comparative study of the adolescent's concepts of his parents and teachers.' *Educ. Rev.*, 14, 226–32.

YEAGER, T. C. (1935): *An Analysis of Certain Traits of High School Seniors interested in Teaching.* New York: Teachers College, Columbia University.

ZELIGS, R. (1948): 'Children's intergroup attitudes.' *J. Genet. Psychol.*, 72, 101–10.

ZUNICH, M. (1962): 'Relationships between maternal behaviour and attitude toward children.' *J. Genet. Psychol.*, 100, 155–65.

INDEX

Index

163

Index

Index

Index

Index

Index